JOY
that
LASTS

Resources by Gary Smalley

Bring Home the Joy
For Better or For Best
Hidden Keys to a Loving, Lasting Marriage
How to Become Your Husband's Best Friend
If Only He Knew
Joy That Lasts
Making Love Last Forever
Keys to Loving Relationships (18 videos)
Secrets to Lasting Love (5 videos with R. Greg Smalley and Michael Smalley)

Discover the secret to a marriage
so fulfilling it will lead to...

JOY

that

LASTS

REVISED EDITION

Gary
Smalley

With Al Janssen

ZondervanPublishingHouse
Grand Rapids, Michigan

A Division of HarperCollins*Publishers*

Joy That Lasts
Copyright © 2000 by Gary Smalley

Requests for information should be addressed to:

📖 ZondervanPublishingHouse
Grand Rapids, Michigan 49530

Library of Congress Cataloging-in-Publication Data

Smalley, Gary.
    Joy that lasts / Gary Smalley with Al Janssen.--Rev. ed.
       p.   cm.
    Includes bibliographical references.
    ISBN: 0-310-23322-4 (hardcover : alk. paper)
    1. Spouses--Religious life. 2. Marriage--Religious aspects--Christianity.
I. Janssen, Al. II. Title

BV4596.M3 S63 2000
248.8'44--dc21
                                        00-023351

This edition is printed on acid-free paper.

All Scripture quotations, unless otherwise indicated, are taken from the *Holy Bible: New International Version.* NIV. Copyright © 1973, 1978, 1984 by International Bible Society. Used by permission of Zondervan Publishing House. All rights reserved.

Interior design by Laura Klynstra Blost

Printed in the United States of America

00 01 02 03 04 05 /❖DC/ 10 9 8 7 6 5 4 3 2 1

To Norma Jean Smalley,
who partners with me in allowing
Christ to fill us with his grace.

GARY SMALLEY

To Jo Ann Janssen.
Our joy is that together
we are being conformed
to the image of Christ.

AL JANSSEN

To protect the identity of those I have counseled, I have changed the names and circumstances in many stories. In all cases, however, I have attempted to convey the essence of the experience and communicate as accurately as possible the underlying principles at work.

CONTENTS

INTRODUCTION
This One Thing

OF THE MORE THAN fifteen books I've written, this one is the most important—which is why, after fourteen years, I have to rewrite it.

Millions of people have viewed the *Keys to Loving Relationships* videos and read marriage books such as *If Only He Knew; For Better or For Best;* and *Making Love Last Forever.* I've taught many helpful techniques for intimacy, such as LUV Talk (Listen, Understand, and Validate), meaningful touch, learning the incredible differences between men and women, the language of love, dealing with unresolved anger, and much more. All of these are invaluable tools that equip couples to enjoy a healthy relationship.

This book is different in that it's not really about marriage—yet, it has everything to do with a great marriage. The message I originally wrote in 1986 is for everyone, for it contains the essence of life as God meant for us to live it. It's for the married and never-married, the divorced and widowed, newlyweds and senior citizens. I decided to rework the message within the context of marriage because if *both* husband and wife will live out this message, I *guarantee* they will have a more fulfilling relationship.

Please note: I am *not* promising a trouble-free marriage. Nor will a couple necessarily be happy all of the time. They likely will need to use the tools I've laid out in various books and videos to improve their communication or better understand their differences. However, this book lays the foundation for everything else I teach.

The title of this book is *Joy That Lasts*; it's not *Happiness That Lasts*. I believe happiness is often a by-product of joy. But when a couple suffers the loss of a child, or a spouse is laid off from a job, or a basement is flooded during a heavy rain, they will not be happy, to be sure. Yet during these times, they can still experience joy and a quiet internal peace that somehow the situation will work out for the best.

Happiness is a *sometimes* emotion that comes and goes according to one's circumstances. Joy is far deeper. For those who possess joy, it is not merely an emotion, but a part of their character. It is not something we can manufacture, but it is the result of a deep spiritual encounter. This joy is available to all who seek it, and when both husband and wife have it, it is the glue that keeps them together and growing in their relationship.

Although this book is not about tips and techniques, I believe you will discover many helpful ideas for your marriage. But more than that, I hope you will learn how to live life at the deepest level, the way God intended for it to be lived. I want to provide hope and anticipation that good is coming your way— guaranteed! I want you to understand the pain and see the hopelessness I felt at the lowest point of my life, and then realize that my worst experiences turned out to be for the very best.

This book, especially chapter 2, is my story. When you read what I did, I hope you will take a similar road toward spiritual fulfillment. You don't have to go through trials like mine to discover the truth I found. However, you no doubt have suffered, or will soon experience, your own trials. The road I propose will give meaning to your suffering.

For Norma and me, this message is the secret of our life, marriage, and work. Thousands have found this joy. It certainly is not unique to me—it spans the centuries back to the early church.

To illustrate the power of this joy that lasts, I begin with two stories that may seem to present impossible circumstances But there is no situation that can block the penetrating power of joy.

CHAPTER ONE

Yes, You Can Have Joy

NANCY BRAMLETT WAS MISERABLE—TRAPPED in an abusive marriage with no hope of improvement. For her, divorce wasn't an option, but shopping was.

It was summertime in Memphis and Nancy, with her friend Linda, were on a mission. They started with clothing. Hopping from mall to mall, and boutique to shop, they tried on all the latest styles and colors. Midday, there was a lunch break at a trendy café or bistro. Sometimes she'd think wistfully about brief times spent living in Boston and Miami, where she could shop at Jordan Marsh or Bonwit Teller. Those happy memories and the thrill of making their latest purchases covered up the pain, at least for a few hours.

In time, Linda and Nancy became bored with clothes. So they visited Ethan Allen and Kacey's and any number of quality antique shops looking for the perfect dining-room set or a unique accessory for the living room. Late in the summer, with closets full and extra furniture stored away, Nancy held a giant garage sale and cleared out the items she no longer wanted, making room for winter fashions she was planning to buy that fall. During a break between customers, she wondered why all her new purchases left her satisfied for only a day or two. Why, when she had so much, did she need more? At a time when so many acquaintances considered her lifestyle glamorous, why was she so unhappy?

Certainly anyone would be envious of the phone calls that came during the months between her husband's seasons in the National Football League? "Is John there?" said the voice.

"We're about to eat dinner," Nancy answered.

"Elvis wants you guys to come over." Immediately, Nancy turned off the oven, put the food in the refrigerator, and called a baby-sitter. John and Nancy then hurried over to the Graceland mansion for dinner with longtime friend Elvis Presley. Afterwards, they might play a football game at the high school field a couple of miles away, or Elvis might rent the old Memphien Theater so they could watch a movie without being disturbed by a myriad of fans. Sometimes in Graceland, Nancy would slip away for a moment to call her mother to check on her sons, Andy and Don.

Isn't this the American dream? For seven years, your husband is a star linebacker in the NFL. After injuries force him to retire, his competitive drive is channeled into business, where he is even more successful. You have all the financial resources you need; you have two children you love dearly. But while your husband provides well financially for his family, he can't give what you want most—some attention, a little time, a sense that you are important to him. In a word, Nancy wants to feel *loved*.

All the pain of her marriage came to the surface one evening in a bar when one of the secretaries from John's office grabbed Nancy's arm and hissed, "Your husband tried to get me to go to an apartment with him this week. I thought you ought to know about it." Nancy stared at the woman, her mouth open wide in disbelief. Humiliation engulfed her. Her face felt as if it were on fire. She wanted to vanish beneath the table. By the pity she saw in the woman's eyes, Nancy knew she was telling the truth.

She turned to her husband and his stunned look of surprise confirmed the accusation. "She's lying, Nancy," John quickly blurted. "Can't you see she's just making the whole thing up?"

Nancy turned and ran for the parking lot. Sobs convulsed her as she reached their car. John was right behind her. "Nancy, listen to me. That woman's lying. How could you be stupid enough to believe her?"

"No, she's not lying!" Nancy shouted back. "I want to know what she's talking about. What apartment? How many other women have you asked to go there with you? Doesn't our marriage mean anything to you?"

"Sure it does. I told you, she's making it up. It never happened, Nancy, I swear it."

They drove home in silence that night, speaking no more about it, and the next morning they acted as if nothing had happened. But Nancy now knew for sure what had been happening on those nights when her husband didn't come home. She'd assumed he passed out from drinking, and because he didn't come home, she was managing to avoid another ugly abusive scene, so common when he was drunk.

How could Nancy live in such an awful situation? Isn't this a prescription for divorce? No one should have to endure such pain. Was there any hope that John could change? Surely after years of addiction to alcohol, barroom fights, battles with police, and abuse of his wife, he wouldn't change.

Perhaps you'll be surprised to learn that John and Nancy celebrated their fortieth wedding anniversary in the summer of 1999. After fourteen years of problems, they found the secret of a happy marriage. It started with Nancy, and John followed a few months later. It didn't happen because Nancy changed John; for years she'd tried to reform him—and only failed miserably.

Rather, both found *joy* to fill their inner emptiness. And once their inner needs were met, they were finally free to begin to give to each other in their marriage. Today, they work together, helping others find the same joy.[1]

The joy this couple found is the theme of this book. And if you're tempted to think that Nancy's experience is just a happy exception, consider the story of Bo and Gari Mitchell.

The request seemed innocent at the time. Bo Mitchell listened carefully as his friend, the president of a local bank, explained what he needed. Would Bo take out loans for two mutual friends—one for $110,000, the other for $90,000—to help their real estate company through a short-term cash-flow problem? Bo qualified for the loans. The need seemed genuine. And, in fact, the loans were soon paid back and the matter forgotten. Until seven years later, when Bo received a call from the Federal Bureau of Investigation.

Now Bo stood before a federal judge, awaiting sentencing. What he'd done, an act known as "straw borrowing," was illegal—a felony. Though he'd ignorantly broken the law, he'd been pressured to plead guilty to the offense. The prosecutor assured him that he would probably get off with probation— that was their strong recommendation. After all, Bo was a respected businessman who had never been in trouble with the law. Besides, no one had lost any money.

As he waited for the judge to speak, Bo glanced behind him at his wife, Gari, sitting with their two children in the courtroom. He smiled, remembering their conversation the previous evening. "Bo, did you know that what you were doing was wrong?" Gari had asked.

"Of course not!" he'd answered. "Do you think I would have done it if I knew it was illegal?"

---

[1] Story taken from unpublished manuscript by Nancy Bramlett with Joyce Tart Morton.

Gari had put her arms around him and said, "Bo, I want you to know that I've never met a man with more honesty or integrity than you. Whatever happens tomorrow, I'm proud of you. We'll get through it."

Not long before, Bo's wife had endured her own trial. She'd gone into a severe depression, and Bo had flown her to Mayo Clinic, where a chemical imbalance was found in her brain. She'd been on medication since, and the depression had lifted. He had supported her through that trial; now she was standing by him in his time of testing.

The sharp rap of the gavel brought Bo back to the present. After a few perfunctory questions, the judge announced his decision. "I understand that this crime was not Mr. Mitchell's idea, and in fact, he was invited into this crime at the request of his friends. However, I believe in general deterrence. Therefore, the most lenient I can be in this case is to sentence you to spend eleven months in the federal penitentiary. Case dismissed."

Bo stood there absolutely stunned. *The judge said he was being lenient? This made absolutely no sense.* He felt his wife putting her arms around him, and turned to embrace her. All he could think to say was, "Eleven months. What did I do to deserve eleven months in prison? Why didn't I fight this and take my chances with a jury of my peers?"

Fortunately, Bo didn't have to enter prison immediately. It was the Christmas holiday season, and the court said he could report after New Year's Day. As he started thinking about the time he'd spend in confinement, it occurred to him that he could either rebel against God for allowing this, or he could surrender. He told Gari, "This is causing me to run into the arms of God. I'm going to go in there and be quiet and find out what God has for me."

Shortly before entering prison, Bo received a book called *Joy That Lasts*. It provided a breakthrough lesson. He explains the impact this way: "If you are going anywhere other than Jesus

Christ to get your tanks filled, you will be incredibly disappointed. You will be confused, lonely, and possibly reckless, especially if you look to other people."

Bo says that for years he was a people pleaser. "I put people's needs before my needs, before the needs of my own family. I felt I was ready to explode, I was trying so hard every day to please people." For the first time, Bo was forced to withdraw from people, business, and sports, none of which could now satisfy him. Prison would become a forced spiritual retreat from a fast-paced life of constantly going to the wrong place to refill his tanks.

Today, Bo and Gari believe they have a far stronger marriage than before this ordeal. While many couples experience the breakup of their marriages when one spouse goes through depression, and an even higher percentage divorce when one goes into prison, these two trials brought this couple closer. It wasn't the problem itself that caused them to draw close, but what they *learned* in the trial.

Both the Bramletts and the Mitchells learned how to experience lasting joy. And they found the joy in the midst of awful circumstances. Let's be honest, there is one thing all married couples experience—problems! You can't avoid them. Our lives are filled with things that can cause us stress and drain our energy. Trials can come from work, from financial pressures, from tension among friends, from illness in the family, from problems with kids and in-laws—the list is endless. All of these problems can feel like holes are being drilled in us, draining our energy.

Many of the problems we face are outside of our control. But there is one thing we *can* control—*our reaction to problems.* We can let the stress of life divide us in our marriage. Or we can discover the unending source of energy that allows us to fully enjoy our spouse. The choice is ours.

There's a general assumption within our culture that each person deserves to be happy. Many people look to marriage to provide that happiness—and the divorce rates show how many people lose it, or never find it. I believe happiness is an unrealistic expectation for the marriage relationship, because happiness depends on what happens around us. It requires the cooperation of people and circumstances. Unfortunately, that cooperation rarely happens.

Joy, on the other hand, is completely different. Joy comes from within, and doesn't depend on people or circumstances. As you read through these pages, you'll discover that either now or in the future, your own problems may be only relatively mild, or they may be as serious as Bo's or Nancy's. But the exciting truth is that whatever "fire" we go through, God is able to use the fire to making us stronger and more loving—when we discover the *source* of lasting joy.

Over the years, I have discovered five keys to experiencing this joy. Together Norma and I have practiced these five keys for more than twenty years. They've been tested in numerous trials, some of which I will tell you about in this book. These truths have never failed us. Yet early in our marriage, I violated every one of them.

For a long time, I really didn't know what I was missing because I was totally immersed in my work. For me, everything meaningful in life was tied to this ministry. And when it failed me, I was devastated.

CHAPTER TWO

Joy Comes Before a Satisfying Marriage

THE MOST TRAUMATIC EXPERIENCE of my life turned out to be the best thing that ever happened to me and my family.

When I originally wrote *Joy That Lasts*, the story I am about to tell was disguised to protect the identity of the organization and its leader. Today, I can use their real names, but it is important to realize that this story is *not* a reflection on them, but on *my* problems and immaturity.

As a young man fresh out of graduate school, I met Bill Gothard at the church where I was assistant pastor. He had just started a small organization that taught life-changing principles in the Christian life.

Bill's charisma captivated me. Like a modern-day John the Baptist, he called people to return to biblical principles of life. And he lived what he preached. He was totally committed to his work, to the extent that he had decided (at least at that time) not to marry. Accepting his invitation to work for him was the easiest decision I'd ever made.

My wife, Norma, didn't share my enthusiasm. In spite of my excitement, she told me several times she felt I would regret working for this ministry. She thought I was so eager to work there that I was unable to see some things that weren't right for me. But I "knew" better. I believed Bill was a modern-day prophet who had a vision to change America, and *I* was going to help him.

The year was 1968. Six of us manned the ministry headquarters in a suburb of Chicago. We doubled the size of the organization in the first year and doubled it again the next. We could hardly contain our enthusiasm when we realized that everyone in the United States would attend our seminar within fifteen years if we continued at the same rate of expansion.

The team began to reserve major arenas in which to hold meetings. We packed out seminars in Seattle, Long Beach, Chicago, Dallas, and Kansas City. To see entire sports arenas filled as Bill motivated people to live Christ-centered lives staggered me. And then to see people filling our coffers by buying our books and other materials was more than I could believe.

I helped open regional offices in ten cities and hired managers to supervise promotion and registration for local seminars. On the road every month, I interviewed prospective employees, approved office leases, helped negotiate agreements with arenas and convention centers, and conducted motivational seminars of my own for our employees and volunteers.

My most significant memories, however, were not of packed conferences, or of the constant travel and the first-class accommodations. What meant the most were the times Bill and I slipped away to a remote cabin. There we would spend a couple of days praying, developing new conference and seminar materials, and plotting strategies to take our message beyond the borders of the United States to the entire world.

Every few hours we would take a break and toss rocks into a trash can, competing like two kids to see who could make the most shots. Sometimes in the evening Bill would grow tired, and I'd keep him awake, motivated by the thought of testing new material or conducting our seminar in still another new city. People's lives were being transformed by Bill's work, and I passionately believed this movement had to spread as quickly as possible.

Bill was everything I could want in a friend; in fact, in many ways he was like a brother. We shared much more than the vision to help people. Because we were nearly the same body size, we often borrowed each other's clothes. Many times I walked into my office and found a new shirt or tie on my desk—a present from my best of friends.

Sometimes Bill would call me late at night, embarrassed that he couldn't remember who had borrowed his car. I would drive the four blocks to our headquarters to pick him up, and often we'd go out for a late dinner. Inevitably I would have to pay because money meant little to Bill. Frequently he didn't even have his wallet with him. But he was a generous man. When Norma's car was in the shop for repairs, I'd simply go into Bill's office and he'd give me the keys to his car. His door was always open, and I was involved in most of his meetings. As far as a lifework, I couldn't imagine a better situation. I believed we would work together until I retired. I was unbelievably happy.

My wife, however, suffered from neglect. She was at home with two toddlers, and I was absolutely no help. I was on the road as much as half the time, and when I was *physically* home, my mind was engaged in planning and strategizing. There was no question that my family was far down on my list of priorities, but I was too busy to recognize that.

At that time, we only had one car. Many times my wife would drive to the office to pick me up from work. I could see her sitting in the parking lot with our active kids crawling all over the car seats, but I was busy in a hastily called meeting. Sometimes she'd wait for more than an hour, and I didn't even have the courtesy to excuse myself for a moment and go tell her I would be late. My attitude was that she should appreciate the importance of what I was doing. I wouldn't even *consider* leaving a meeting with Bill Gothard until I was dismissed.

My life began to change with a single phone call. Janet, Bill's secretary, said, "Norma's on the phone." I took the receiver and remained standing next to Janet's desk. "Gary, sit down," Norma said in her cheery voice. "I have some great news to tell you."

"I only have a minute," I answered. "We're about to start an important meeting."

"I was just at the doctor."

I froze for a moment. "Is something wrong?"

"No . . . I'm pregnant!"

My knees buckled. I looked around, grabbed a chair, and sat down. We had two children at the time. Kari was five; Greg was three. We had tried for a while to conceive a third child, but I had recently concluded that we were finished having children. I was relieved with that decision, for the demands of work were so heavy that I couldn't imagine another round of changing diapers and getting very little sleep at night.

I tried to hide my feelings. "That's great, Norm," I said half-heartedly. How could I say I was actually disappointed? What had gone wrong? Hadn't she used protection? Didn't she know how busy I was? I didn't need any more stress and frustration in my life.

Michael's birth turned out to be very painful for Norma. She endured eighteen hours of intense labor, and when our son emerged, he was seriously ill. I tried to help with the other kids while Norma cared for Michael. While pressure at work was severe, the staff was very understanding of my situation. I was the one feeling I wasn't doing my part. Then when Michael was two weeks old, we were told that he needed to undergo major surgery in order to save his life. We all breathed a sigh of relief when he came through that trauma. Finally, I could get back to work.

As soon as possible, I resumed a full schedule. I was traveling a lot, and working twelve to fourteen hours a day, plus weekends. While I was aware that Michael still required extra care, I figured Norma could handle it. I was wrong. One evening, when Michael was about a year old, I walked into the house at about eight o'clock and collapsed on my favorite chair. Norma slipped into the chair opposite me. She was crying. "I don't know how to tell you this," she quietly said, "but I can't go on this way anymore."

I sat up, unable to speak. Without raising her voice, she said, "I can't raise three children, one of them a very sick baby, with you gone so much. Our lives are out of balance, and something has to change soon. Quite honestly, you've got to cut down on your work and stay home more."

It was so matter-of-fact. No yelling. No ultimatums. Just a statement that she was at the end of her rope. To this day I'm ashamed to say I wasn't sympathetic. What was *I* thinking as Norma suffered from emotional and physical exhaustion? *How can I possibly tell Bill that I can't work so many hours? Doesn't Norma know that Bill needs me? Doesn't she realize that I'm one of his key leaders?*

And yet, how would it look if my wife wound up in the psychiatric ward of the local hospital? She hadn't said that, but in my heightened state of anxiety, that's what I imagined. Here I was in ministry, helping couples and families, and my own marriage and family were crumbling. How could I continue the same routine when they were suffering? Something had to give.

The next day I trembled as I went to Bill and said, "My wife is unable to handle my schedule. Is there any way I could slow down my travel schedule a little so I could be home more?"

What happened next was the best thing Bill could have done for me. In a sense, he fired me! Of course, it took a while for me to realize what a blessing that was.

By way of context, it's important to explain that a lot of changes had occurred within the ministry. Our headquarters complex was teeming with more than one hundred employees. We were no longer a small, intimate family. It hit me one afternoon when I walked into Bill's office and asked for his car keys. Without looking up from his paperwork, he informed me that we now had a new policy. "The staff will no longer borrow each other's cars," he said, and with that I was dismissed. In the days that followed I was also informed that I had to knock before entering Bill's office and that I was no longer needed in some important meetings I had been attending just a few months earlier.

Like a jealous suitor, I was hurt and confused by this sudden change in our working and personal relationship. I kept wondering what I had said or done to induce this kind of response from Bill.

In the week that followed I learned "through the grapevine" that some members of the new management team did not approve of my qualifications and were concerned by the amount of access to and influence I had with Bill. So almost overnight they had gotten me moved away from the fireplace into a cold, damp corner.

So I shouldn't have been surprised when Bill relieved me of my management responsibilities. He didn't actually terminate me; rather, he told me I would now report to his father (whom I didn't like at all) and help monitor the financial cash flow of the organization.

I had wanted to be relieved of some of the responsibilities of travel. Instead, I had no travel responsibilities at all. I wanted to reduce my hours, but not at the expense of losing all of my leadership authority. Besides, I was a minister, not an accountant. I hated working with numbers. Now, instead of dreaming about seminar content and strategizing about the growth of the movement, I was at a desk every day, poring over purchase orders and invoices. I was keeping records and paying bills. Just when my desk was almost clear, Mr. Gothard would bring me another box of bills and receipts from "The Traveling Team."

What made it worse was hearing team members say how much they missed me. They'd say things like, "Wish you were going with us to southern California. We're going to Disneyland before the seminar begins." As they drove off, I could only think, *My life is over. They don't need me.*

It seems incredible to admit this today. But I was slipping into a deep depression over the situation. I was mad at Michael—his very existence was somehow responsible for the loss of my position. I was mad at Norma—she wasn't strong enough to handle the pressure. I even entertained the thought that she had orchestrated my being fired. There were some mornings when, after I got up, I went right back to bed and pulled the covers over my head. There was nothing I liked about my life.

But I *was* home. And I *did* start doing things to help Norma. I changed diapers and fixed meals and helped clean the house. An amazing thing happened as I did these things, even though I didn't *feel* like doing them. I realized that being a father and a husband was more rewarding than traveling around the country in a jet and helping other husbands and wives improve their marriages. It was more fun actually loving *my own family* than teaching other families how to love.

One day I walked over to Michael's crib, gently picked him up, and said, "Little Mikey, I want to thank you for bringing me home to my family. You are a special gift from God. Like an angel, God brought you into our lives to wake me up and make me realize that the corporate world doesn't hold a candle to my family."

That's not to say I was out of the woods emotionally. For a long time I was unable to talk about my struggles. Bill had been my spiritual confidant. He was so respected in the Christian community, I didn't feel I could seek counsel from anyone who knew about our work without sounding like a disgruntled employee. It was even difficult to express my fears to Norma.

It took nearly two years and a career change before I understood the answer. In the process, I began to realize a tremendous truth:

*T*rials *can be our greatest experience,*
for they can lead to the source of lasting joy.

Through this devastating experience I discovered the secret to a life so fulfilling that today it is almost impossible for circumstances to rob me of my joy for any length of time. Further, when I found this joy, I enjoyed my family more. Best of all, when Norma and I both experienced the source of lasting joy, our marriage became incredibly rich and zestful. Until then, I never realized how much I was missing in my marriage.

Bill and my job had satisfied me for almost nine years, but when things started going wrong they became like acid, eating holes in the walls of my life until everything fulfilling and meaningful had drained out. Through that experience I learned the secret to keeping my cup filled. There was one source that would not only fill it, but cause it to *overflow!*

No doubt, you are facing difficult circumstances, or you will face them one day. Some of you are hurting because you've been rejected by someone you love. Some of you have climbed over fences to find greener pasture but found only a desert instead. Some of you have followed a rainbow only to find the pot of gold is an illusion. And some of you are worried that the good life you enjoy may evaporate right before your eyes.

As incredible as it may seem, those who recognize themselves in any of the above circumstances are on the brink of the most important discovery of their lives. In fact, problems are the tools that help us fill our lives with lasting joy, peace, and love. But most of us do not even recognize the tools, much less know how to use them.

Five Things Every Marriage Needs

So where did I go wrong? How could I wind up in such despair? My derailment occurred because I was looking for happiness, not joy. There is a major difference between happiness and joy. Happiness in life is transitory, dependent on circumstances. Joy continues regardless of trials. That's especially true in marriage. When a couple discovers joy, they are free to enjoy marriage the way it was designed by God. And they are able to endure all that life throws at them.

Even though I was involved in a highly respected ministry, I failed because I didn't know the source of joy. What's more, my marriage struggled as a result. I believe I violated five principles. These are five things every individual (not just married people) needs in life, but we tend to look for them in all the wrong places. But when we have these five things, we are able daily to experience indescribable joy.

FIRST, *I Needed an Energy Source to Recharge My Spiritual and Emotional Batteries*

I was looking to Bill and to my job for my energy. Everything that gave my life meaning and significance came from my friend and my work. When I was with him, I was high. When I was on the road planning an event, my life felt important. On those occasions when I was not getting what I needed from work, I would look to Norma to make up the difference. But she was busy with three kids, so my expectations often weren't met. I didn't realize that neither my job nor any person would provide the lasting fulfillment I needed. That had to come from another source.

SECOND, *I Needed Someone to Whom I Could Pour Out My Heart and Talk to About Anything at Any Time*

You might naturally think my wife would be that person, and Norma tried to help. But I knew she had expressed concerns about my being involved in this work, so I didn't feel free to completely open up to her. And the problem with having only one really close friend like Bill was that when *that* friendship changed, I had no one else to turn to. What I didn't know was that I *did* have this type of friend. He was waiting for me to open up to him, but it took me a long time to realize it.

THIRD, *I Needed to Understand My Emotions, For They Were Warning Lights Telling Me I Was in Trouble*

I didn't know it at the time, but there were numerous indications that I was in trouble. My anger at Bill and the ministry was a big one. Fear of the future was another. Loneliness should have been a clue that I was expecting too much from Bill. Depression was a major warning sign that life wasn't cooperating with my expectations. But I didn't understand my emotions, and so I suffered far more than necessary.

FOURTH, *I Needed to Know That There Is Meaning in the Trials We Endure*

The Bible makes a promise—though it is one we don't really want to claim—that we all will endure trials. Trials are an inevitable part of life. But I was totally unprepared for this trauma. Norma couldn't help me either, because my trial had caused a crisis in her life. There was no way then that Norma and I could come together and gain understanding of the situation. Now I can look back and tell you that this crisis was one of the *best* things that happened to me and Norma. I would never want to go through it again, but I truly wouldn't trade what I learned either. The message of this book, the joy that Norma and I discovered, is a direct outcome of my crisis.

FIFTH, *I Needed to Have a Shared Mission with My Wife That Was Beyond Us, One That We Could Strive for Together*

You no doubt noticed that Norma wasn't a part of my work with Bill. So often we segment our lives, and work stays distinct from family. But by leaving Norma out of this part of my life, I lost something of great value. Fortunately, today Norma and I have combined our talents—and we are a team. You may see me in front of a crowd at a conference, but believe me, without her supportive work, there is no conference. The joy we get out of working as a team is incredible, even though it's not always smooth sailing.

This Joy Is Available to Everyone

You may be reading this and thinking, "I sure do want this joy, but my spouse isn't going to cooperate." Let me say right now that this joy is available to *you*, regardless of your spouse. In fact, even if your spouse *wants* to meet all of your needs, he or she will never fulfill your every longing in life. This is something that must be discovered individually. And if your mate doesn't cooperate, you will still gain personally, and so will he or she.

However, a marriage is strongest when both a husband and wife are emotionally and spiritually healthy. When they both have a source of joy that doesn't depend on the other, they are then free to give of themselves to each other. That's when marriage becomes truly exciting.

I never understood this myself until I lost almost everything of value. During my search for meaning and purpose after my devastating experience I discovered several biblical tools that turned my tragedy into triumph. In the following pages I'd like to help you identify and learn to use them in your own life. These tools help us build up our self-worth; regulate for our benefit our negative emotions such as anger, worry, fear, and envy; and equip us to go on a treasure hunt to find the "gold" that is buried in every trial.

The message that God intends us to live in a perpetual oasis may encourage us for a season, but before long we *will* run into trials, and with them comes the dry, barren desert. Crossing a desert unprepared can be deadly. My prayer is that this book will help you prepare for inevitable desert experiences and show you how to find the true source of refreshment. This discovery will lead you to the source that is always running over, never running dry. I missed out on this refreshment for years because I kept trying to find something tangible that would finally satisfy me. I learned instead that even *having it all* wasn't enough.

CHAPTER THREE

Having It All Isn't Enough

THE FAMOUS ACTOR OPENED the door and invited me into his New York City penthouse. In his living room, whose windows took in the city skyline, was a fireplace, and on the mantel of that fireplace was a statuette, the only memento of his illustrious Hollywood film career.

Having never seen an Oscar up close, I spent a moment reading the nameplate. This actor had won Best Supporting Actor at the Academy Award presentations a year earlier. "I've spent all my life working for that," my host said. "I really believed that if I won this award, it would give my life meaning. It would tell the world that I am somebody. And, I'd finally be happy."

The actor paused for a moment, a catch in his throat. I waited. Finally, he asked the question that had prompted him to call and ask me to fly two thousand miles to meet with him. "So, Gary, why am I feeling so miserable?"

This lonely man, who'd only recently suffered through his third divorce, voiced the lament of our culture. How is it possible to be so successful, and at the same time so unhappy? Why does it seem that the more someone has—things that most people aspire to have, such as fame, huge financial resources and the things they buy, a gorgeous spouse—the less happy that person often is?

First of all, that kind of sadness is not unique to the rich and famous. Almost everyone in our culture is affected by the same problem—in fact, those who don't have wealth and success are often just as miserable chasing after the elusive American dream. They simply can't believe that possessing those things won't make them happy.

I had to reach bottom to discover the secret of fulfillment. My failure at work had produced in me a severe depression that lingered for several weeks. Norma tried to understand why I was depressed, but it didn't make sense to her. However, my problems were causing a crisis in her life, and the answers she found had a profound impact on me.

Never underestimate the power of a woman who has yielded her life to God. She not only has strength, but a special, radiating beauty. Norma had that glow during our courtship and when we were first married. After several years of marriage, however, her power and beauty had started to fade, and she blamed me for her lack of fulfillment.

When we'd moved to Chicago so I could work with Bill Gothard, we had left a wonderfully supportive church. In Chicago, we never found the right church for our family, and as a result, Norma began to feel more and more isolated. Furthermore, she felt lonely because I was gone so often and rarely available for meaningful conversation. She *did* have the children; ever since she was a little girl Norma had wanted to have many children, and being a mother was very fulfilling for

her. But with three preschool youngsters, she needed the support of a loving husband.

I wasn't aware of it at the time, but my insensitivity to our
family caused a serious crisis in my wife's life. For a year after
Michael's birth, Norma prayed about the imbalance in my life.
At one time, early in our marriage, she would have tried nagging
or shouting to get my attention. But those strategies rarely had
much effect. Now, with her expectations about our marriage and
family shattered, she began spending more time with God.

The more she went to God with her needs, the more Norma
realized that God wanted to have a special friendship with her;
he was fully capable of meeting her needs—and that included
trusting him to work in my life too. She thought about the
example of Sarah, the wife of Abraham. Sarah was so distraught
over not bearing a child that she took matters into her own
hands and made things worse. Norma realized that she needed
to speak to me about my imbalanced life, but to do so in such a
way that God was free to work things out in his way. And even
if I *didn't* change, she began believing that God still was faithful to meet her legitimate needs.

As Norma began to experience a greater intimacy with God,
a feeling of calm and peace entered her life. It didn't change her
situation; I was still out of balance. My wife truly believed that
this problem had to be confronted. But how? As she prayed,
she realized she had to face me and courageously tell me the
truth of her situation. When she finally did so, she spoke calmly,
without histrionics. The strength of her spirit made a major
impact on me—enough to cause me to go to Bill to ask about
changing my job.

Norma's example also forced me to begin searching for
answers. For several months during my crisis at work, I frequently woke up at three or four o'clock in the morning with
my stomach churning like a stormy sea. I desperately wanted to
understand why I was experiencing such misery. If the

Christian life that I believed in and spoke about was true, why was I so unhappy? Why couldn't I rise above this disappointment and move on with my life?

One morning I awoke at four o'clock with the familiar pangs of anxiety engulfing me. To keep from disturbing Norma, I quietly slipped out of bed and tiptoed down the hall. My six-year-old son heard me. "What are you doing, Dad?" Greg whispered.

"I'm going downstairs to study," I told him.

"Can I go with you?"

After pouring Greg a cup of juice I sat down with him at the kitchen table and admitted to him that I was going through a struggle and couldn't seem to find the answer. He listened and tried to understand. "Greg, there has to be a reason why I keep getting my feelings so hurt. Do you remember the time we went fishing and you lost that big trout? You cried and I had to hold you for a long time?" Greg nodded. "That's a little like how I've felt for the past few weeks. I feel like I had a trophy fish right at the edge of the boat—but it got away. I feel such a deep sense of loss that I can't feel joy anymore."

Greg didn't fully understand, to be sure, but talking to him helped me crystallize my thoughts. Perhaps if I could explain to a six-year-old boy what I was feeling, I could go on to understand it myself. "Greg, I think I've been making the same mistake over and over. Maybe that's why I'm so miserable." I looked at his nearly empty cup of juice and suddenly had an idea. "It's like my life is a cup, and until recently it was filled with joy and peace and love. But lately a big hole has been drilled in it and all the life has drained out. Instead of joy filling my cup, anger and fear and hurt feelings have taken its place."

"But what made that hole?" Greg asked.

As I talked, I realized I had been expecting my relationship with Bill to keep my cup filled. I grabbed a notepad and drew a picture. "I think it's becoming clearer to me! Greg, tell me if this makes sense."

I drew as I talked. "As I think about it, Greg, I'm not look-ing for life just in a relationship; actually I'm looking for life in at least *three* different places. And fulfillment from these three places floods into my life through a network of hoses and faucets. The problem is, someone has turned off the spigot!" I showed Greg the picture, and he said he understood.

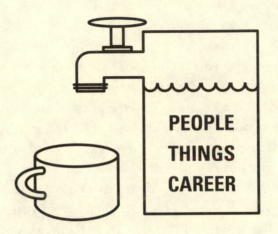

*F*or the first time I began to realize my major mis-
take: I was expecting to find fulfillment in people,
things, and career. Not only did I no longer receive
fulfillment from these sources, it was as if the satisfac-
tion they once had given me was now destroying me.

That early-morning conversation with Greg changed my life. For the first time I began to understand why my emotional and spiritual life had been like a small sailboat on a large lake. On nice days with gentle breezes I would skim across life's sur-face, refreshed by the wind and invigorated by the spray. But when the storm clouds came (and they always do), I had no safe harbor to sail to and no anchor strong enough to help me ride out the storm. The lake that once provided pleasure and fulfillment suddenly became life threatening.

In recent years, I've found a new way to express this experience that makes a lot of sense to me. It has to do with power sources. Imagine that I have within me a rechargeable battery. This battery gives me the energy I need to get through each day. But inevitably, my battery runs low on energy, and when it does, I need to plug it in and recharge it. In my own personal life, and through working with people I'm trying to help, like the famous actor in New York, I find we tend to plug into one of three sources: people, things, or career.

People—We Can't Control Them

For the first thirty-five years of my life I thought people were supposed to make me happy. My wife, children, friends, relatives, boss, fellow employees—all were part of a group I felt should charge my battery. This belief contributed to my problem with Bill. I enjoyed our friendship so much that I began to expect it to continue unchanged forever. In a subtle way, I shifted from following Bill's leadership to expecting him to cooperate with *my* goal of enjoying our unique friendship. I became more interested in our meetings than in the goals of the ministry. Preparing material and planning new strategies, while at first utilized as a means to help more people, became ends in themselves—ways to spend time with Bill.

I had similar expectations of my family. I wanted them to appreciate the great movement I was privileged to be part of and to serve me by submitting their desires to the goals of this great work. I had no problem expecting my wife and children to wait an hour outside in the cold until I finished a meeting. After all, I was helping to bring a spiritual and physical revival to our country. What could possibly be more important than that?

It was years before I realized, with grief and embarrassment, that I'd selfishly expected my wife and kids to serve *my* ambition. No wonder Norma and I weren't receiving much joy in our lopsided relationship.

I see this attitude frequently among young couples. Take, for example, a woman who dreams for years about finding "Mr. Wonderful." She believes this man will fulfill her deepest longing for intimacy. She pictures him sitting next to her on an overstuffed love seat in front of a warm fire, his arm around her, talking for hours. She sees them discussing their plans for the future, their next vacation, and how they'll redecorate the living room. She knows he will diligently fix things around the house, keep her car running smoothly, and be there to support and encourage her when she is discouraged. She often thinks of her husband-to-be as a waterfall cascading into her life, a never-ending source of fulfillment that will make her life overflow with meaning.

This woman doesn't know she's setting herself up for the very heartache she's trying to escape. It doesn't take long—usually no more than a few weeks into the marriage—and she begins to realize that her husband, in many ways, can't or won't cooperate with her expectations. The relationship she expected to bring her security may actually make her *more insecure.* Her husband may be the type who notices every attractive girl who walks by. He may be so wrapped up in his work that he shows little interest in her work or activities. He may be too tired to fix her car or make necessary household repairs. Even his interest in touching her may seem to have only sexual motivations.

Before long this woman, who once had so many dreams, begins to feel used and taken for granted, almost as if he had hired her as a maid. Not only is he not charging her battery, but his insensitivity has started to drain her emotional resources. If not corrected, she will eventually lose whatever amount of love, happiness, and peace she had when she entered the marriage.

When her husband fails to meet her needs, she may think of an alternative: "If my husband isn't going to meet my needs," she reasons, "I'll have a family. Children running around the house are just what I need to be fulfilled!" Too late she discovers that children, rather than charging her battery, have an amazing capacity to short-circuit her power cord.

A man also enters marriage with many expectations. He pictures how his wife will respond to him. Each day she will comment on how gifted he is as a lover, husband, and father. Without question, she will prepare delicious meals every night and always respond warmly to his sexual desires.

Soon he, too, discovers that not only is she unable to charge his battery, but being around her produces a brownout. Like her, his insecurity increases, and he may begin to think he married the wrong person. He may even begin to look around for another woman he thinks will better meet his needs and become his ultimate "battery charger." An affair for either spouse may well produce a momentary charge—but it doesn't take long before there's a major power shortage as the spouse attempts to keep the affair a secret. Affairs are a lot easier to start than finish. Repairing the damage from an affair is like trying to rewire an entire house after it's been hit by lightning, blowing all the circuits.

Husbands and wives are by no means unique here. Most everyone experiences frustration because they look to *people* to fulfill their expectations. Children may long for greater love from and better communication with their parents. Parents may feel "taken advantage of " by their children. Employees often feel that employers do not care about them as people. Employers may feel that employees have no sense of loyalty or gratitude. And many Christians feel betrayed when certain "super-Christians" succumb to temptation and turn out to be just as human and just as prone to failure as anyone else.

In the book of Proverbs we read, "Hope deferred makes the heart sick" (13:12). Many husbands, wives, children, employees, employers, and friends put their hope for fulfillment in other people, which eventually leaves them empty and frustrated inside. Researchers like Albert Bandura and other sociologists believe this looking to other people to supply our happiness is a major cause of many social problems. Their research on anger and acts of violence related to anger shows that a key contributing factor is "frustrated expectations," the same thing that leads to divorce, runaway youth, suicide, battered mates, kidnapping, and drug and alcohol abuse.

I am grateful I finally began to see this principle, because my unrealistic expectations of others kept me from gaining the fulfillment I was desperately seeking. No matter how "perfect" they might be, people would never be able to charge my life battery.

But if that is true, where then can we turn?

Things—We Never Get Enough

When people don't satisfy us, we often look to money and the things money can buy—cars, entertainment systems, computers—the list is endless.

For those who live in the United States, the first place most couples expect to find fulfillment is in their own home. John and his wife, Joan, went through emotions similar to mine. Each expected fulfillment from the other. When they didn't find it there, they thought a new home might help. They built a beautiful house on several acres in a suburb of San Francisco, but they still had trouble getting along. John felt they needed a change of location, so he built a beautiful mountain cabin. That didn't solve the problem, however, because they fought just as well in their cabin as in their spacious San Francisco home.

It seems that few couples are content without a proper home. We're concerned about the neighborhood, the number of bathrooms, the view from our living-room windows, and whether we have appropriate furnishings and coordinated interior decorations. Whether we rent or own or live in an apartment or a sprawling split-level, we expect pleasure and satisfaction from our home. We even feel cheated if we're not living in the right location. But *getting* our dream home can cause more anxiety than not getting it. Often we end up worried about how we're going to make our mortgage payments, how or where to add another room, and what security system to install to protect our investment.

When Norma and I finally bought our first house five years after we were married, everything about it—the smells, the fresh paint, the new neighbors—excited us. But after the initial thrill wore off, we noticed how loud the neighbor's dog barked and how irritating the continual loud music was that came from their patio. What's more, they did nothing to control their dandelions, so their weeds quickly spread to our grass.

As we settled into the routine of living, our house became ordinary. Our friends' new home was more spacious and had more conveniences. We began to think we, too, needed those things. But the more things we bought, the more things needed fixing. The bigger the house, the bigger and more expensive the problems and the more time and effort they consumed.

I admit I enjoyed fleeting moments of satisfaction from our home in Arizona, but it frustrated me more than it satisfied me. My garage door broke an average of twice a year. The hinges on the back gate fell off. Swarms of aphids set up housekeeping on our roses. Dust from the expansion of our family room kept circulating through the house after construction. My lawn was always dying, either because I gave it *too much* water or fertilizer or *not enough*. My sprinkling system broke whenever a car pulled too close to the edge of the lawn. And I lost the war against weeds.

At one time, my dream was to own a home on a golf course. Norma and I finally realized that dream with the purchase of a beautiful house inside the grounds of a country club. The first morning I woke up to the sounds of a tractor mowing the green outside our house—at 5:00 in the morning. I didn't want to get up at 5:00 in the morning. Why couldn't they wait until 8:00 or so? And while the view was beautiful, when I would sit outside there were always people walking by, or workers manicuring the grass, or sprinklers running. I hated it!

In my travels across the country and overseas I've visited in many homes and found happy people and miserable people in both small apartments and spacious dwellings, which suggests to me that *where* we live has relatively little to do with our level of happiness.

In most marriages, one partner will be tight with the budget—he or she will be a saver—and the other will be a free spender, confident that somehow the funds needed to pay that latest credit card charge will appear miraculously before the bill arrives. It's a frequent source of tension in marriage. While this issue must be addressed, I'm talking about the underlying attitude both spouses have about money. The free spender is usually looking for happiness from what he or she spends. The saver is expecting security from the amount of money in bank accounts or mutual funds. Neither approach provides lasting energy, and certainly neither produces lasting joy.

I took a large cut in pay when I parted company with Bill, so I was thrilled when I had a business opportunity that promised to yield at least $200,000 in the first year, and perhaps twice that amount the following year. Norma and I quickly thought of things we "needed"—a microwave, a new phone system, a sophisticated stereo system, a new washer and dryer. Our house suddenly seemed far too small and outdated. We drove around town and found a beautiful two-story home overlooking a lake. The price was only half of the "minimum" amount we thought I would earn. We began to figure ways to borrow the money for this house in anticipation of our windfall income.

Fortunately the bank never considered our loan request. The amount of money we actually received paid only for a grandfather clock we had bought in anticipation of moving into the new house. Every day that clock was a grim reminder that we could not move out of the home we no longer liked.

One of the toughest times in my life was the first time I achieved significant financial reward. After one failed attempt, I was involved in an incredibly successful infomercial. Four times a year for the next three years I received huge checks. The moment you come into a lot of money, your mind tricks you and your eyes grow larger and you see things you "need" that you didn't know you needed before. Some good friends of mine gave me this solid piece of advice: "Gary, don't live on this windfall. Live on what you earned before you made this income."

Money does not provide lasting fulfillment, nor is it the key to the door marked "The Overflowing Life." My personal observation of people, plus my own experience, has led me to conclude that there are very happy people who have no money, and very happy people who have lots of money. And I know very unhappy people with no money, and very unhappy people with lots of money. Yet many of us live as though cars, campers, and boats bring lasting enjoyment to life.

We see this attitude displayed especially at Christmastime. Millions believe the holiday ad campaigns that tell us which things will bring happiness. But after all the gifts are opened, many of us slide straight into discouragement, even depression. Year after year the pattern repeats itself; new possessions cannot satisfy us for long.

Failing to find lasting joy in a house or other things, many people begin to look outside the home to a place where they can "have it all" while they "get away from it all." They plan a dream trip to Hawaii to enjoy the sun and surf or to Colorado to enjoy the snow and skiing. But all too often it's simply that— a dream.

Vacations can be enjoyable, but the possibilities for disaster are endless—bad weather, lost traveler's checks, a vehicle breakdown, canceled flights, stuffy motel rooms. Our first trip to Hawaii illustrated this beautifully.

I was scheduled to speak in a gorgeous hotel on the north side of Kauai. We looked forward to a week of sunbathing and sight-seeing on the island paradise. But it rained every day we were there. The travel brochure conveniently withheld information about the island's average rainfall, which, where we were staying, was reported to be 425 inches a year!

Things we least expect can ruin a vacation we've anticipated for months, or even years. Like the time we planned a special ski trip with our relatives. First, we lost the key to our shared apartment and nearly froze while we tried to find the manager. Then my niece got a severe nosebleed as we prepared to make our first run down the mountain. And on my second trip down the slope, the stomach flu attacked me unexpectedly. As I tried to hide in the woods to relieve my stomach cramps, I slipped and slid forty feet through the trees. My son, Greg, laughed uncontrollably while I spent thirty minutes trying to dig myself out of the snow and clean myself up.

Because I travel so much, people often tell me they envy me; they think traveling is exciting. What they do not realize is that traveling drains my battery. The headaches of arranging itineraries and purchasing tickets, rushing to make connections, experiencing yet another delayed flight and another round of lost luggage, added to fatigue from jet lag, uncomfortable beds, and flat pillows, drain away any joy that traveling might otherwise provide. If you enjoy your family, every day on the road is another day away from those you love the most. Most people who look to travel for fulfillment end up woefully disappointed.

Places, whether homes or vacation spots, are like a mirage. To a person thirsting for fulfillment, they look like a quenching pool of water. Yet once we reach them we find only sand—and the ten thousand other tourists who beat us to the spot!

Things, like people, cannot energize for long. If you think they will, just wait until something breaks—and see how much energy you have then. So what's left? Disillusioned by relationships or things, many people look for fulfillment in what they do.

Career—We Can Never Climb High Enough

Our job or career is important because of what it supposedly provides for us. Jobs may provide status—most men in large part gain their identity from what they do—and they also provide money, which allows you to maintain a certain lifestyle. But even those who have significant incomes often aren't satisfied.

Work is not always fun, especially when we have to do the same thing over and over again. Besides, jobs rarely live up to our expectations. When we reach a position for which we've striven, there is usually so much pressure connected with it that it loses much of its glamour. Like owning a big home, the responsibility can consume all our energy.

Most of us focus on what we expect to gain from our job: money, security, promotions to new positions, benefits, or fulfillment. We may attain these things for a time, but no job is secure. We must continue to perform well, or we will lose our job. If the company is sold, the new management may decide it no longer needs us. The economy may slump. The marketplace may change. And all the while we grow older. Nearly all of these factors are outside of our control, but they undermine our position nevertheless.

Les worked for thirty-three years as a lineman for the phone company. He thought he had the ultimate in job security. Because of his seniority, he would be one of the last to be laid off; and a layoff was inconceivable because he worked for the largest telephone company in the world—AT&T. Who could have anticipated that Ma Bell would be forced to break up? Only three years away from retirement, Les learned his job would be phased out. There are no guarantees in life.

Over the years I've discovered something interesting while working with professional athletes. Most of us think these sports figures enjoy security with their large, multiyear contracts and the glamour of their positions. Instead, however, I often found them disgruntled when they did not perform well, when they weren't playing as often as they felt they deserved to play, when they were suffering from a nagging injury or couldn't get along with their coach. If a six- or seven-figure contract with a professional sports team is a guarantee of happiness, why do so many professional athletes demand to be traded or want to have their contracts renegotiated? And why do they have so many problems with drugs, alcohol, and divorce?

Not all professional athletes fall into this trap, to be sure. Recently, as I was working on this book, I heard of a professional baseball player, Jeff King, who left the Kansas City Royals in the middle of a season because of an injury, with three million dollars left on his contract! All he had to do to collect the money was to finish the season on the disabled list. But Jeff viewed it in a different light. "We could have helped a lot of people with that money," he admitted. "But it's just not right to take money for nothing. People might think I'm stupid, but you have to do what's right."[1]

What's more, Jeff was ready to leave the spotlight of professional sports. He observed that "I never liked people looking at me and pointing me out and wanting my autograph. I never was comfortable with their expectations of me." And so he walked away from the "good life" and settled his family on a remote ranch in Montana.

Another recent example is the testimony of basketball superstar David Robinson after his San Antonio Spurs won their first National Basketball Association championship. In an article in

---

[1]Quoted in Ron Cook, "This Was Jeff King," *The Gazette* (May 30, 1999), Sports, 7.

Sports Illustrated, he wrote, "Everybody thinks the trophy and the ring are the ultimate things, but as valuable as they are, they're just *things*. They'll wind up on a shelf somewhere, but the experience of winning them, the journey, will be right here in my heart forever."[2] Unlike the Academy Award-winning actor, David Robinson had learned that fame and fortune don't give meaning in life. No one can escape the truth that *position* does not provide lasting security and satisfaction. By the time I started to understand this principle, I had worked in both menial jobs and in what I considered the ultimate in a challenging leadership position for a large ministry. I couldn't imagine going any higher, short of replacing Bill Gothard, which I had no desire to do. Yet even at "the top of my game," I finally realized that this position could not provide the continual joy and peace I desired.

Many within the Christian community fight the same temptation. They, too, are prone to accepting the myth that they can find fulfillment by achieving position. Some Christians would love to share the limelight with a television personality or be able to sing like their favorite Christian recording artist. Believers who hold secular jobs may long to be able to work for a ministry organization or a church. They presume that if they were working in a Christian environment they would surely not be bothered by the problems and pettiness they encounter in the secular workplace. Working in that type of environment, they think, would be like having a perpetual "quiet time."

Unfortunately, even in a ministry setting, certain things about a job can still leave us lacking lasting fulfillment. One reason jobs do not satisfy is that they all have at least one thing in common: *Work!*

How many men and women have sacrificed their family life for a higher position only to discover that the position they

---

[2]Quoted in David Robinson (with Phil Taylor), "Mission Accomplished," *Sports Illustrated* (July 5, 1999), 40.

sought didn't fulfill their expectations? And in the process they lost their relationship with their children. Instead of the fulfillment they were looking for, what did they find? Hurt feelings, anxiety, fear, stress—the very things they were hoping to avoid.

Others are obsessed with work now because of some perceived comfort they look forward to experiencing in the distant future. There's a story I heard that expresses this well. An American businessman was at the pier of a small coastal Mexican village when a small boat with a single fisherman docked. Inside the boat were several large yellowfin tuna. The American complimented the Mexican on the quality of his fish and asked how long it took to catch them.

"Only a little while," the Mexican replied.

"Then why didn't you stay out longer and catch more fish?"

"This is enough to meet my family's needs."

"But what do you do with the rest of your time?"

"I sleep late, fish a little, play with my children, take a siesta with my wife, Maria, stroll into the village each evening where I sip wine and play guitar with my amigos. I have a full and busy life, senor."

The American scoffed. "I am a Harvard M.B.A. and could help you. You should spend more time fishing and with the proceeds buy a bigger boat. With the proceeds from the bigger boat you could buy several boats. Eventually you would have a fleet of fishing boats. Instead of selling your catch to a middleman you would sell directly to the processor, eventually opening your own cannery. You would control the product, processing, and distribution. You could leave this small coastal fishing village and move to Mexico City, then Los Angeles, where you would run your expanding enterprise."

The Mexican fisherman asked, "But, senor, how long will this all take?"

"Fifteen to twenty years."

"But what then, senor?"

The American laughed and said, "That's the best part. When the time is right you would announce a public offering and sell your company stock to the public and become very rich. You would make millions!"

"Millions, senor? Then what?"

"Why, then you would retire. Move to a small coastal village where you would sleep late, fish a little, play with your grand-kids, take a siesta with your wife, and stroll into the village in the evenings where you could sip wine and play your guitar with your amigos."

Other areas breed insecurity as well. Many people think they would be fulfilled if they could lead a great cause, work full-time helping people, become a media celebrity, cut a record album, win a political election, or write a book. Consumed by the excite-ment of these activities, some ignore the potential cost in time or finances, loss of privacy, and weighty demands from supporters.

One of the highlights of my life was when I taped my first infomercial. The celebrity host was Dick Clark. I thought this was the ultimate—life didn't get any better than this! Just how long did that feeling last? Two days. Then I plunged into deep discouragement. I had expected this experience to be a lot more fulfilling. But it was no big deal. I was plugging into the wrong power source.

We need to refocus our expectations on a totally different source. It's not enough to stop expecting fulfillment from people, things, and career. After my talk with Greg that morn-ing, I realized where life did *not* originate. But I still did not know how to plug into the *genuine* source of life. I couldn't imagine how or why I had failed to learn such an important truth during my years of seminary and church involvement, or in my association with Bill and his seminars. If *I* didn't know the answer, who did?

My search for answers began with God himself. My prayer for help was nothing more than a whimpering cry: "God, teach me what I'm missing. What am I failing to understand?" What I discovered was that I was using the wrong extension cord. People and things and career were like trying to use a 110-volt power source with an appliance designed for 220 volts. We are designed for 220 volts, but we are trying to charge our batteries with 110 volts, and it doesn't work. The plugs and outlets don't even match!

More than twenty years ago I first prayed that prayer for help, and I can honestly say that the years since have been the most fulfilling, adventurous, and overflowing I've ever experienced.

Here are three reasons why my battery is almost always fully charged today:

1. While negative emotions such as hurt feelings, envy, jealousy, anger, depression, lust, fear, and worry can still crop up, I make a conscious effort not to allow them to linger.
2. Positive, life-giving emotions have replaced negative emotions. I regularly experience love for and from others, and my inner joy and happiness do not depend on God's creation. I have an inner calm and contentment—a peace of mind—that I never used to experience.
3. I've learned how to use the painful, emotionally difficult experiences of life to benefit me and those around me.

A fulfilling life has nothing to do with people, things, or career. When the *true* source of fulfillment floods us, a deepening sense of security accompanies it, assuring us that the source of life cannot be yanked away.

Once our life is charged by this source, we are truly free, for the first time, to enjoy God's creation—because we can appreciate it *without* depending on it for fulfillment. This was my mistake—expecting life from God's creation. We live overflowing lives because the *source* of life, instead of the *gifts* of life, brings us contentment. The question I had was how to find and tap into *this* power source.

Where Are You Looking for Fulfillment?

Separately, husband and wife, rate your personal happiness at this moment in each area, from 0 to 10, with 0 being totally dissatisfied and 10 being totally satisfied:

1. My mate meets my physical and emotional needs.
2. My closest friends remove all sense of loneliness.
3. My children are a constant source of joy.
4. Our home is everything we want.
5. We make all the money we desire.
6. We have everything we want.
7. We are planning (or have taken) the perfect vacation.
8. I have the perfect job.
9. I am involved in satisfying work.

Now review your answers.

Are people, things, and career meeting your needs:
___ Yes   ___ No   ___ It's hit-and-miss

Would you like to be rid of the pressure of depending on God's creation to charge your battery? That's what we'll be addressing in the remainder of this book.

CHAPTER FOUR

Finding the Unending Power Source

Do you know what it's like to be married to someone who's not looking to you or anything else but God to make him or her happy? Such a person rarely gets her feelings hurt. A man like this doesn't get upset very often. Sure a man or woman can be hurt or upset for a moment, but once they change extension cords and are plugged into the right source, they experience peace and contentment. How does this happen? By finding the source of power that never runs low.

That was the question I faced in my personal crisis: Where would I find lasting fulfillment? Learning that I had looked for contentment in all the wrong places for so many years left me empty. Even after I prayed and asked God to show me what was missing, I sensed a hollow darkness inside. Then suddenly, as if someone had switched on the emergency floodlights, I began to realize why I was so discouraged.

It happened in my office on a Monday morning. I had no motivation to begin work, and I was too hurt and disgusted to attend the weekly staff meeting. I had just received a letter and a check for sixty dollars from a minister I had met a few days earlier at one of our seminars. I reread the letter and felt a wave of embarrassment. The pastor asked me to use the money to buy a new suit. He had noticed that I wore the same suit for three consecutive years; he said his motivation for sending me the check was 1 John 3:17: "If anyone has material possessions and sees his brother in need but has no pity on him, how can the love of God be in him?" How could I explain to this well-meaning man that I didn't need a new suit? Besides, I probably earned three times his salary. I should have sent him money!

Intrigued by his comments, I reached for my Bible and read the five short chapters of 1 John. Bible reading had become no more than a daily ritual for me during this stress-filled time. For weeks I'd read my Bible without gaining any spiritual insights. But this time my mind was unusually alert as I tried to sense even a glimmer of truth that might help me. The words in chapter two stunned me: "Anyone who claims to be in the light but hates his brother is still in the darkness. Whoever loves his brother lives in the light, and there is nothing in him to make him stumble. But whoever hates his brother is in the darkness and walks around in the darkness; he does not know where he is going, because the darkness has blinded him" (1 John 2:9–11).

Over and over I read those verses. The word *darkness* precisely described my experience of discouragement and lack of enthusiasm. I knew that walking in God's light meant walking in God's love; however, I had never equated my lack of love for Bill with hatred. Maybe others could see it, but I had missed it. Not only did I not love Bill, I had actually developed a deep anger toward him. Left to fester, my anger had turned into a form of hatred.

Could this be true? I felt I was too spiritual and mature to actually hate someone. I'd never yelled at Bill or tried to hurt him in any visible way. Yet, according to God's Word I was walking in *darkness*, not in light, because I did not love my brother.

Though perhaps not evident on the outside, my angry thoughts and bitter spirit proved that I hated Bill. And though my hatred wasn't affecting *him*, it was destroying *me*. I could not function in more than the routine activities of my job and life. No wonder I didn't sense God's love or have a desire for spiritual things. I was slipping into darkness, and I wasn't even conscious of it.

Rarely has Scripture so overwhelmed me. I slid out of my swivel chair and onto my knees. "God, it's hard for me to admit it, but what you've written in this verse is true of me," I prayed. "Now I understand why I don't sense your presence and why I'm walking in such confusing darkness."

I left the office knowing that my conflict was not with Bill. By allowing anger to remain within me unresolved, I was fighting a law of God. Blaming Bill had kept me from seeing my own immaturity and lack of love. In my anger, I had set myself up as his judge. I had examined the evidence and mentally pronounced a guilty verdict. Yet I could not possibly understand all that it took for Bill to lead a ministry. And even if I had known, by judging him and hating him I was superseding God, the only true Judge. I recalled James 4:12: "There is only one ... Judge, the one who is able to save and destroy. But you—who are you to judge your neighbor?"

It was time to resolve this. I went home and suggested to Norma that I go away for several days to be alone with God. She encouraged me to go, for I'd been impossible to live with. If it would bring me out of my depression, she was eager to give me the time. So I grabbed my Bible, a jug of water, and a pen and paper and headed over to our ministry's vacant rental house a half mile from our home.

During the next several days, I began to learn the secret of having my battery fully charged. Away from telephone, radio, television, and all other interruptions, drinking only water, I prayed and read through the New Testament. "Lord," I prayed, "I'm willing to read through your Gospels and as many other books in the Bible as it takes for you to teach me the secret of finding the abundant life you promised."

Luke 11 was the first chapter to jump out at me. When I read about the disciples asking Jesus to teach them how to pray, I thought, *Aha! Maybe this will help me find the answer.* So I prayed, "Lord, teach me how to pray." If I asked God, through prayer, to help me discover the secret to fulfillment, and if God indeed answers prayer, then he would show me the secret I so desperately needed.

The exciting thing concerning the secret I was about to learn was that it had nothing to do with the people or things around me, or with my position. Furthermore, it had nothing to do with my earthly accomplishments, my level of education, or my financial condition. It had everything to do with understanding Jesus' words: "I have come that they may have life, and have it to the full" (John 10:10).

What I learned from Luke 11 and Luke 18 is the greatest secret to life.

Discovering God's Best

The first clue came in Jesus' parable in Luke 11. Can you see in this passage what helped me understand fulfillment?

> *Then he said to them, "Suppose one of you has a friend, and he goes to him at midnight and says, 'Friend, lend me three loaves of bread, because a friend of mine on a journey has come to me, and I have nothing to set before him.' Then the one inside answers, 'Don't bother me. The door is already locked, and my children are with me in bed. I can't get up and give you anything.' I tell you, though he will not get up and give him the bread because*

he is his friend, yet because of the man's boldness [or per-
sistence] he will get up and give him as much as he needs.
So I say to you: Ask and it will be given to you; seek and
you will find; knock and the door will be opened to you.
For everyone who asks receives; he who seeks finds; and
to him who knocks, the door will be opened."

(LUKE 11:5–10)

I acted out this parable in my mind to try to understand it. I pictured myself as the person who went next door to borrow three loaves of bread for my unexpected visitor. I began to knock on my neighbor's door at midnight. "Don't bother us," I heard him shout. "We're all in bed. I can't get up and give you anything." But I knew that if he did not help me I would only have to pass the word around the community the next day and he would be ostracized. My neighbor was a good friend. We'd fished together and shared many meals. Our children played together, and I couldn't say how often we had borrowed things from each other. However, those were not the reasons he eventually helped me at such a late hour. He got up and gave me as much as I needed because of *my persistence* and in order to *protect his reputation.*

Jesus went on to make the application for us. Why are we to continually ask and seek and knock? *Because God's reputation is at stake.* I could pray, "Lord, what's the secret to the abundant life you promised in John 10:10?" I intended to keep asking this question until I got an answer, and I knew God *would* answer because he will not be shamed. I was asking, and God promised I would receive. I was seeking, and God promised I would find. I was knocking, and God promised to open the door to understanding.

From this parable I learned two crucial principles: First, God will not be shamed. He guards his Word and reputation as did the neighbor portrayed in the parable I'd read. Second, God is faithful to answer the bold, persistent prayers of his children.

Recognizing God's Faithfulness

As I read the next parable, another truth about prayer emerged.

Which of you fathers, if your son asks for a fish, will give him a snake instead? Or if he asks for an egg, will give him a scorpion? If you then, though you are evil, know how to give good gifts to your children, how much more will your Father in heaven give the Holy Spirit to those who ask him!

(LUKE 11:11–13)

If we humans know how to give good gifts to our children, just think about the almighty God of the universe, our heavenly Father. He promises to give his very Spirit to those who ask. I suddenly realized this was what I was seeking. This was the life God had promised! Life was contained in his Spirit living within me. If I had the Holy Spirit, I would have love, joy, peace, patience, and all the other fruit of the Spirit (see Galatians 5:22–23). Ephesians 3:19 states that to *know* the love of God is to be "filled to . . . all the fullness of God." I know it is God's Spirit *alone* who fills my cup and charges my battery.

This wasn't new to me—I'd heard it hundreds of times. What was new was *how* to gain God's Spirit and keep that relationship alive.

During those days, I went to God as a child goes to his father. As a hungry son seeking bread, I stated my requests:

- I asked to experience God within me and that I might no longer expect anything other than God to fill my life.
- I asked for healthy family relationships and that Norma and I and our three children would love each other and be an example to other families.
- I asked for knowledge and wisdom to be the best possible husband and father.

- I asked God for a friend who could guide me further in this truth. I needed someone who would help me resolve my inner turmoil regarding Bill and help me live an obedient Christian life.
- Finally, I asked God to let me guide others, particularly by preparing me to do more personal counseling so I could share my insights from God.

Even though God promised to be faithful, I couldn't keep myself from presenting one little stipulation. I asked, of all the people who might be that "special friend" to help me grow, that it not be Bill's father. I had sensed his concern for me, but I was so angry at his son that I couldn't stand the thought of getting any assistance from him.

The answers to my prayers began almost immediately. First, Bill called me into his office a few days later to discuss how we might resolve the struggle we were having in our relationship. As I stood before him, I wavered as to whether or not I should tell him about everything I had been learning and feeling. Just when I was about to open up and express to him what was on my heart, Bill said, "Gary, I think you need to talk to someone besides me about what's been going on." Then he told me he had arranged for me to spend extra time with his father.

I could have resigned on the spot. I was confused and upset with God. I felt as if I had asked for a fish and been given a snake. I couldn't understand why the one person I specifically wanted to avoid had become a major part of my week.

Though I sensed that God's Spirit was changing me, I had to struggle to keep from walking out of the room. Yet those days of prayer and fasting had been so meaningful to me that I prayed instead. "Lord, even though I'm confused and upset, I am *not* going to try to figure this out. I'm willing to let you prove your faithfulness in my life."

That afternoon I started meeting with Mr. Gothard, and almost overnight God used him to pull me further out of my discouragement. More than I ever thought possible, Mr. Gothard understood Bill as well as my conflict with Bill. Instead of lecturing me, he listened and prayed with me. In the time I spent with this man over the next few weeks my attitude changed from resentment at having to meet with him to feeling rewarded because we were meeting together.

This represented a major turning point in my life. I began to realize that God was not giving me a scorpion or a snake. He was *faithful* in answering my prayer. Like a loving father, God knew what I truly needed. I could relax and trust God even when I didn't understand what he was doing. My confidence in God grew by leaps and bounds as I continued to knock on his door for my other requests.

God had answered my prayer about finding a close friend to help me work through the situation with Bill, and soon I began receiving answers to my other requests as well. I had prayed to be a godly husband and father and to learn to keep my family in harmony. Without my lifting a finger, God answered that prayer by opening a door. A good friend and pastor I had met through the ministry called and asked if I would consider doing three things in his church: First, he wanted me to become a better husband and father so I could teach others out of my own life experiences. Second, he wanted me to develop a ministry to families. And third, he asked me to begin a counseling program at his church.

While Norma and I prayed about this exciting opportunity, an almost identical offer came from another pastor in California. Now I had not only one chance to learn more about my family and family ministry, but two!

This dilemma fascinated me, and I've seen it happen many times since. God is so faithful that he often gives several answers to a single request. Those two offers showed me how far I had slipped into discouragement. Before digging into the Gospel of

Luke, I had questioned whether I would ever see any answers to prayer again, or whether I would ever be of service to God. These opportunities showed me that our ways are never hidden from the Lord and that regardless of our circumstances, God has a task for us to accomplish for him.

Seeing the things I had prayed for come together reassured me of God's faithfulness. I hadn't sent out dozens of résumés looking for a job, nor had I asked Mr. Gothard to become my friend. Yet in both cases God, in his own way and timing, had honored my requests, just as he said he would in Luke 11.

Norma and I decided to accept the first offer—to serve as family pastor at a growing church—and we prepared to move our family to another state. As I began to plan my departure from the ministry, I felt a renewed love for the people I was leaving. Even though my conflict with Bill had been devastating in many ways, I found I still loved him and knew, finally, that God had used our problems to draw me closer to himself. In fact, I began to understand that if I had never gone through that experience I might never have discovered the depth of God's faithfulness or become so meaningfully related to God.

But God had taught me another truth concerning prayer that has become my primary tool for discovering answered prayer.

Persistence—A Secret to Answered Prayer

During the days I camped out in the Gospel of Luke, I listened intently each time Jesus spoke about prayer. In Luke 18 Jesus introduced two parables by telling the disciples that "they should always pray and not give up" (Luke 18:1). The first story Jesus used is now one of my favorites; in it lies a fantastic secret to effective prayer. Here's the scene:

Imagine a wicked, unrighteous judge assigned to a small city in Israel. He has no respect for God or people. He is disgruntled because he would rather be in Rome enjoying the pageantry, games, and parties. Instead he's stuck with a bunch of farmers, shepherds, and religious fanatics. Every day people line up to present their grievances to him—and he passes judgments according to his particular mood.

In the line of people stands a widow with no one to look out for her best interests or to protect her. Her situation appears hopeless. Others take advantage of her, but she has no legal rights. Although many think that she is helpless, she knows the secret to gaining justice. The first time she presents her petition to the judge, he brusquely dismisses her. But she does not give up. After coming before him repeatedly, she finally gains legal protection; the judge concludes that he will see to it that she gets justice, "so that she won't eventually wear me out" (Luke 18:5).

Jesus urges us to listen carefully to the story of this unrighteous judge. Jesus pictures an important truth people need to understand. It was the woman's *persistence* that brought results. Jesus went on to ask in conclusion to his parable, "Will not God bring about justice for his chosen ones, who cry out to him day and night? Will he keep putting them off?" (Luke 18:7).

Following my retreat, I imagined myself coming every day as the widow did and lining up before God. From Luke 11, I learned that God was loving and that God would be faithful to his children. From Luke 18, I learned to get into God's prayer line every day, a practice I have followed since 1975.

When I line up to pray, my petitions fall into three categories: First, I ask for God's will, and for what God promises to give his children—love, joy, and peace through the Holy Spirit—that's fulfillment. Second, I pray about the needs of my family. And third, I pray for the needs of people around me.

After we moved away from Bill and his ministry, one of my major needs was to be free of resentment toward him. I knew it was wrong for me to feel betrayed and to desire revenge, but I could not shake myself loose from these emotions. Every day for two years I applied the principle from the parable in

Luke 18 and prayed as I jogged: "Lord, I'm in line again, along with many of your children. I must admit how upset I still am with Bill. I don't know how you're going to do it, but I know you're going to free me. Maybe this is the day! And if not today, perhaps tomorrow!"

After two years of getting in line every day and requesting that freedom, it finally came. A man from my church approached me with an article from a counseling magazine. "This article describes a problem I'm having," he said. "Would you read it and then could we talk about how to solve my problem?"

Even though this man was looking for help for his own problem, the article perfectly described *my* conflict with Bill. It also provided the final pieces of information I needed in order to resolve the conflict completely.

The article explained in depth about Bill's leadership style and strong drive to achieve. It also explained why my personality type reacts to and feels hurt by this kind of leadership. Bill had a large organization to run and didn't have the time to explain all of his business decisions to me. Finally I saw why I couldn't expect *him* to repair our broken relationship.

At last I had the information I needed in order to be able to love and forgive Bill instead of letting all my emotional energy drain away by being bitter toward him. Once I stopped long enough to *understand* his personality and leadership style, it was easy to forgive him. That day I stepped out of that prayer line and never again needed to get back in it to discuss this particular situation. My resentment toward Bill disappeared, never to return again.

Shortly after reading that counseling article and experiencing God releasing me from my anger, I drove to one of Bill's seminars and had a great visit with him. Some of Bill's mannerisms that once caused me to become angry reappeared, but this time, rather than bristling and wanting to separate myself from him, I listened and felt genuine love for Bill and respect for his work. I actually wanted to pray for a special blessing of God on his life. That's when I knew I was really free! In fact, to this day we continue to see each other and talk on the phone. I realize now that my problem with Bill was *not* Bill's problem. It was *my* attitude and lack of knowledge and maturity.

God is not only faithful to answer our persistent prayers for spiritual needs but for physical needs as well. An example of God's faithfulness in taking care of everyday practical concerns involved my daughter, Kari. Every night for approximately two years the two of us stood in line asking God to provide a car. I was earning significantly less than I had during my ministry with Bill. Now our family station wagon was on its last legs and full of rattles. The engine was unreliable, and I had wired together the broken springs in the front seat on the driver's side with coat hangers. I did not have the money to replace the car and did not want to go into debt again, but I never mentioned the need to anyone else.

One afternoon while working with a businessman, we took a break for a hamburger—and he decided to drive my car. When he sank down in the seat and leaned toward the door he asked if this was my only car. I said it was. "This is pathetic," he said. I laughed and agreed with him, but I was caught totally by surprise by what he said next. "Tomorrow I want you to go down to any car lot in town and pick any car you want. I'll pay for it."

That kind of experience has been repeated again and again in all areas of need. I never presume on God's timing, and I never expect satisfaction from any material thing he gives. Yet time after time the reality of God's provisions for my physical needs reminds me that he is indeed my source of life. Even when it comes to things like misplacing my wallet or keys, it's fun to get in line and watch God resolve the "little" things.

That sense of wonder at praying about our needs and watching God provide in surprising ways has continued to this very day. When we moved to Branson, Missouri, I prayed about the kind of house I wanted for the family. One day I asked a friend if he knew of any property. He told me of a farm outside of town that included a house and a barn. I immediately drove out and found the owner at home, very upset. She told me the property had been sold, only to have the buyer change his mind. Her anger turned to excitement when I told her it was exactly the kind of property I was looking for. We agreed on the terms that same day!

Norma and I love our home. It is exactly what we prayed for. But it isn't what brings us our main joy and satisfaction. After all, it's just wood, stone, and glass. But the home is a constant and visible reminder that God loves us and provides for us.

What's exciting about all this is that any child of God can experience the joy of trusting God. I've learned that I can't take pride in what God does for me, because it is *God's* faithfulness, not my spirituality, that makes the difference.

Depending on God for Lasting Life

The trials I underwent in Chicago left me humbled, alert, and convicted. I became childlike, completely dependent on Jesus Christ for both life and direction—the exact position he wanted me in. But many of us have a hard time believing God cares so deeply for us.

As we were driving our packed station wagon out of the Chicago area on our way to a new life in Texas, Norma asked me to pull over to the side of the busy highway. I couldn't understand why she wanted me to stop, but I drove onto the shoulder and stopped. Norma jumped out of the car, threw her arms into the air, and yelled, "I'm free! I'm free!"

I frankly couldn't share her excitement, and soon after we arrived at our new assignment, I learned that the church had decided to pay me $5,000 less than the salary they'd promised when we accepted their offer. Norma wasn't as upset as I was; she fully believed that God was with us and would meet our needs. With an ache in my heart, I got in line each day, asking God to make up the difference in salary. I had no idea how to make any additional money, and I couldn't see how we could cut our expenses much more than we had already done. But as I waited each day in line, I had a growing peace that God would meet our needs.

One day, an envelope arrived in the mail from a longtime friend. In it was a check for $5,000 along with a note that said, "God has really blessed me this year and I wanted to share his blessing with you!" Why me? Why $5,000? That experience had never happened to me before, and it has never happened again.

Within less than a year, we encountered another major problem. It concerned a leader of the church and his sexual orientation. Norma almost laughed when she realized the new problems we faced. It was like God was saying, "You think you had problems before? Wait until you see what's ahead." We realized that so many people want to escape from their circumstances, whether it's a difficult marriage or an impossible job, believing the next situation has to be better. Well, it's often worse!

Here's the thrilling discovery we made: While the circumstances we faced were challenging, *we had joy.* Our experiences in our new home and ministry didn't have a devastating effect, because of what we'd learned in Chicago. Now that Norma and I were seeking joy in Christ, we both were finding more fulfillment in our marriage and family. For the first time, Norma knew I preferred her and the children over my work.

There was still a desire to be involved in ministry beyond the local church where I was serving. I prayed about this, asking the Lord to give me chances to speak that wouldn't interfere with my need to be with my family. And invitations started arriving. Before I would have simply accepted them; now I brought these opportunities to the family and we voted. There were a number of churches in Texas where I spoke. The whole family would travel with me on Friday, and we'd camp or spend a night in a hotel with an indoor pool. These were fun and memorable times. I began to relax about my ambitions and enjoy the family.

Some people may object, saying that these experiences aren't necessarily from God. Maybe it's not an important question for the small things in life, but when people ask God for fulfillment, peace, joy, and love, and these gifts come in lasting amounts, I think that's worth shouting about! And aren't those really our deepest needs? God is faithful to provide what we need when we get in his line. In the same way a child asks a parent for candy or a new toy, we can petition God for the "small things." If he doesn't give them, perhaps they aren't really needs. But God will fulfill his specific promises, such as those for abundant life (John 10:10) and inner peace (John 14:27). My point is that we are all free to stand in line and ask for those things that we know are in accordance with God's will.

A Final Lesson on Prayer

In Luke 18:18–30, Jesus spoke the words that were later to serve as the basis for the famous quote of Jim Elliot, the missionary to the Auca Indians who was martyred in Ecuador: "He is no fool who gives what he cannot keep to gain what he cannot lose."

Jesus promised the disciples in Luke 18:29–30 that anyone who seeks God's kingdom above home, mate, brothers, sisters, parents, and children will receive many times more *at this time*, as well as receiving eternal life in the age to come. But how does putting God first help us in our everyday problems?

Like many of us, Donna needed to learn to put God first in everyday living. She had progressed from anger to hatred to apathy toward her husband, Dave, because of an affair he'd had. She was so disgusted that she did not speak to him for days. Donna was surprised when her pastor showed her that her hatred and judgmental attitude were just as bad as the things Dave had done to her that had caused her hurt. Until she saw the log in her own eye, she could not possibly forgive her husband. Donna humbled herself by admitting her own sin. She also learned to pray for her husband and to wait on God to change him.

Over the next several days, a new love for her husband and a previously unknown sense of calm seeped into Donna's soul. She even started doing special things for him. As the weeks went by, Dave noticed the change in her behavior. Captivated by the beauty of her peacefulness, he finally broke down and asked what had happened. When Donna confessed her judgmental spirit and explained her new dependency on God, Dave expressed his desire for the same peace and joy. Together they went back to the pastor, who helped Dave discover what Donna had found. They became one of the most radiant couples in our church, all because Donna escaped from the darkness of her anger and began walking in the light of her new dependency on God. She saw the truth, grabbed hold of it, and found lasting fulfillment in knowing God personally.

Enter into the Joy!

Dave and Donna found the same joy Norma and I have. We entered into this joy by going to the Lord rather than to his creation.

Continuing with the battery analogy, I came across a powerful reminder of this truth in the letter to the Galatians. Reading in Galatians 1:10, I saw my problem with Bill Gothard in a new light: "Am I now trying to win the approval of men, or of God? Or am I trying to please men? If I were still trying to please men, I would not be a servant of Christ."

I realize now that I was seeking to win the approval of a man. I was out of balance. Norma, however, was seeking to please me, and I was ignoring her need. Both of us were frustrated. We were attempting to have our batteries charged with 110-volt power.

Now contrast that verse with Galatians 2:20: "I have been crucified with Christ and I no longer live, but Christ lives in me. The life I live in the body, I live by faith in the Son of God, who loved me and gave himself for me."

Galatians 2:20 represents for Norma and me the right power source—220-volt power! It's no longer *we* who live, but *Christ* lives in us. We no longer are trying to get our life from people and things and work, but rather we get our life *from God.* Once we began to live Galatians 2:20, our marriage was revitalized.

So how does this work? Every day, whenever I get a negative emotion that makes me aware that I am trying to draw energy from a source other than God, I mentally take my 110-volt cord and unplug it and drop it by the side of the bed, or by my chair, or in the car—wherever I happen to be at the time. Then I take the 220-volt cord and plug it into myself and raise it up to God through Jesus Christ.

I make this transfer by prayer. For example, I may wake up in the morning and find I'm worried about a meeting later that day. The emotion of worry immediately leads me to pray, "Thank you, Lord, that I'm worried this morning, because it reminds me that I think I can't live without this person's approval, when in reality I have you—and you are all I will ever need. Everything else, including this person's approval, is simply overflow. I now drop the cord of seeking approval from another person and raise my real power cord to you, knowing you will give me all I need today."

God has an unlimited number of outlets. Jesus Christ is like a transformer; he takes the power of God and puts it in the amount we can individually handle. I plug into Jesus so I can have life and have it more abundantly. Basically, whenever I have negative emotions, I change cords! My expectations are now from above, not from this earth. And the Bible promises that when we seek first the kingdom of God, all other things are added (see Matthew 6:33). Norma and I would agree: Does God ever know how to charge a battery!

Here's the beauty of this truth. Using the 220-volt picture—that is all the energy I really need. But by letting God charge my battery, I often find he gives me *more* energy than I need—330 or 440 volts. And what do I do with that extra energy? I give it away! I don't need more than 220, so I give away the overflow to others—my wife, my children, whomever it is God brings into my life.

I have found that when I am content in Jesus Christ, I don't need anything on earth. So I am free to love people. People can't give me anything that I don't already have. Norma can't give me what I can only get in Christ. And I can't give to Norma what she can only receive from the Lord. Since we are fully charged by God, now we are free to love and enjoy each other.

I was thirty-five years old when I learned this truth, and it has revolutionized my life. How freeing it is to realize that I have everything I will ever need in life. So what happens then? Because my needs are met, does that mean I give up and do nothing? Absolutely not! By loving God with all my heart and allowing him to meet my needs, now I am free to be used by God in the lives of others.

So here's my challenge to you: Are you plugged into a 110-volt source of power? The checklist at the end of chapter 4 is probably a clue. You can tell if you're disappointed by people, unfulfilled by the things you own, constantly stressed-out by the work you do. If you are feeling miserable, the solution is to change cords.

The way to connect with the 220-volt source God intended for you is to acknowledge that God's creation will never satisfy you. But Jesus Christ will. Go to him and let him know that from this point forward, you will let him be the source of your joy in life.

Now that our lives are completely filled with Christ, Norma and I have found that we actually enjoy the pleasures of life more than we did before, because we don't expect life from them. We have lots of friends, we enjoy traveling to new places, we appreciate a nice home and the various possessions we have. But these things are no longer what we look to for fulfillment; they are simply the overflow of a life filled by Christ. And if we lost all of these things, our lives would still be full because we have the *source* of life itself—a personal relationship with Jesus Christ.

I once heard a story about a man who died and was given a guided tour of heaven by Saint Peter. When they came to an immense warehouse filled with all shapes and sizes of wrapped packages, the man asked Peter what they were. Peter replied sadly, "This is where God keeps all the gifts he intended for his children. These were never claimed." Unfortunately, many today never claim God's promised packages. We leave his gifts in the warehouse of heaven, either because we never ask or because we get out of line too soon.

I don't want anyone to miss out on God's gifts the way I did for so many years—especially the gift of life itself. This new life overflows with meaning so satisfying that the thrill of other pursuits is as fleeting as the momentary excitement of an amusement-park ride.

CHAPTER FIVE

Meet Your Best Friend

WHEN MY WIFE STOPPED fighting me about my obsession toward work, as well as other issues, she unleashed a powerful force in my life, though neither of us understood it at the time.

Independent of me, Norma learned how to get in line and bring her needs to God. Rather than complain to me, she prayed, "Lord, thank you that all I need is you. You know I want a good relationship with Gary and that I want him to spend more time at home. You also know that I'm not very strong physically. I'm so tired that I don't feel I can last much longer under this strain. I'm coming to you with these requests because I know that if I *need* Gary at home, *you* can make it happen. Or you can take away my desire for him to be home. I'm going to stop fighting Gary and instead ask you either to change him or to meet my needs in some other way."

To find God's fulfillment, Norma took steps similar to those I later discovered. She stopped expecting life from me and started looking to God. She realized I not only *would* not, but *could* not, energize her life, so she went to the source of life and asked him to energize her.

The results were startling. I noticed the change almost immediately. When I came home from work, I sensed a calm spirit in our house. Norma's face was peaceful, no longer tense. Instead of the usual harsh words, her conversation was quiet and she was more interested in asking me how my day had gone than in relating her activities with the children.

It was in that context that Norma talked to me about her need for my help. A few days later, I couldn't keep from asking what had happened. "Gary, I got tired of fighting you," she explained calmly. "I realized that I wasn't trusting God concerning our marriage and family, and so I decided to stop complaining and start praying. I've told God that I would like you to spend more time at home, and if I really need that, I know God will make the necessary changes."

Imagine what that did to me. I was instantly convicted that my priorities were wrong. And that wasn't all. Because Norma had changed, I *wanted* to spend more time at home. That was the week I asked Bill to change my job so I could spend more time meeting my family's needs.

What Norma did summarizes the conclusions of the first four chapters of this book. She stopped looking to people, things, and her work, and turned instead to a trustworthy God who answers the persistent prayers of his children. God promises life—and God delivers!

Some may think Norma just disguised her selfishness by asking God to change me instead of nagging me to change. I disagree. I encourage wives to ask God for a good relationship with their husbands and children. That request is not selfish. A good relationship benefits not only the wife, but the entire family, the Christian community, and ultimately our nation and the entire world. It also glorifies God, because a godly marriage is a picture of our relationship with Jesus Christ (see Ephesians 5:22–25).

Once we're into the habit of seeking fulfillment from the world, we won't learn overnight to look to God as the source of life. It took Norma and me several years before looking to the Lord became our natural, first response, and we still catch ourselves focusing on someone or something other than God.

The procedure we follow for obtaining our life from God is not magic. Neither does it need to be kept legalistically, like a scientific formula. These are simply guidelines we have followed from which we hope you can learn and then adapt to your unique situation. God creates us as individuals, not as carbon copies, so put your own fingerprints on the steps that follow.

Step Out of Fantasyland

Many Christians, frustrated by the lack of fulfillment they've found in people, things, and career, have fallen for the deception that God's Word is not entirely true. They live as though the Bible was a book of myths rather than a living and active guide to fulfillment. For them, the hope of gaining lasting love, joy, and peace is like believing Disneyland is real. And attending church is like the temporary thrill of one of Disney's rides. Behind the splashing water, flashing lights, dark tunnels, and dancing figures are only computers and wires and sophisticated sound systems. Christianity is a make-believe world, a ride they take Sunday after Sunday. It doesn't satisfy, but they keep riding, because deep down they *want* to believe it is real.

Others, looking for a greater thrill, switch to different rides, like a new church, a different speaker, or some new teaching. The new ride is more exciting at first, but no more satisfying in the long run.

Some have quit taking the rides altogether. They are convinced that those who say they find fulfillment in the Lord lack depth and settle for the simplistic solutions found in a make-believe world.

How do we escape the amusement-park syndrome where rides go nowhere except up and down, around and around? We begin by admitting that we have sought fulfillment from people, things, or career. These three areas describe our personal Disneyland. The entrance to this amusement park is wide, and many go through it. But Jesus said the gate that leads to life is narrow and only a few find it (see Matthew 7:13–14).

The call to hand over tickets for which we've paid a high price is difficult to obey, but that's the requirement. It's called *confession*. We must admit we've been standing in the wrong line and step willingly into God's line.

Step into Truth

Admitting we've been in the wrong line is only the first step toward facing reality. We also need to move into the right line. That is what the Bible means by *repentance*. It's stepping out of one line and into another. It's turning away from one way of thinking and embracing God's way. It's changing directions, rejecting our former source of expectations and accepting a new source, one that will never fail.

How does this concept actually work in daily life? We've seen that it begins by recognizing Jesus Christ as the power source designed for our lives. But the reality is that the 110-volt power is very attractive. Our lives are full of temptations that pull us *away* from what God says is real life. For example, an area where many of us struggle is with society's emphasis on sexual "freedom." From toothpaste to cars to flowers to resort hotels, we can hardly buy anything that a sparsely dressed woman has not advertised. Because our society is obsessed with sex, lust is a major temptation.

Even though I had a very rewarding relationship with Norma, I was not immune from this temptation. While working in the ministry, I met a woman whom I found very attractive. Yes, temptations like this occur among people who are in ministry and have given their lives to the Lord.

Through months of periodic contact, I gradually developed a strong emotional attachment to this woman. As I gained her confidence she began to tell me about some personal struggles she was having. I empathized with her and wanted to take her in my arms and comfort her, though it never got to that point. When I was honest, I knew I really wanted more than just to hold her.

In time, Norma became aware of this attraction. Earlier in our marriage, she might have reacted in a predictably angry manner. She could have embarrassed me by screaming, "What were you thinking?!" Or she could have threatened me: "You either stop doing this or I'm leaving." Or she could have made me feel guilty, saying through tears, "Do you know how much this hurts? Do you know how humiliating this is?" But because she was now realizing her life came from God, she handled this in a very wise manner.

Norma confronted me one evening with a calm demeanor. "Gary, what you're doing with that woman is not right. You are hurting her. This is against God's law." Norma allowed God to convict me because it was so clear that what I was doing was wrong. What's more, by showing me that I was hurting the woman, it took my attention off of *my desires*—and that pulled the temptation right out of me. It motivated me to want to fix that situation, because ultimately, I really wanted to please God.

During those weeks of temptation I was also learning that people cannot give ultimate meaning to my life. At times I desired to be with this woman, but whenever my thoughts strayed I would confess that she was *not* the source of my life, and I would admit that I was standing in the wrong line. Then I would ask God to make me realize that what appeared to be as harmless and fun as an amusement-park ride was actually a real-life thrill ride that would only crash at the end.

Once I had confessed my desire to have someone other than Jesus Christ fill my life, I would get back into the line that leads to knowing Jesus personally. Although I didn't know it at the time, the Lord was teaching me an important principle about "staying in his line" during times of temptation.

Return to the Source of Joy

Once we have switched lines, how do we continue to experience this gift of life? The apostle Paul writes in 1 Thessalonians 5:16, "Be joyful always." In Philippians 4:4 he commands, "Rejoice in the Lord always. I will say it again: Rejoice!" Paul is so emphatic about this because the word *rejoice* literally means "to return to the source of our joy."

With respect to this other woman, I obeyed Paul's instruction to rejoice by praying, "Lord, *you* know, and I'm just discovering, that this girl will never charge my battery. If anything, she could drain all the energy I have. Not only would I probably wind up in disharmony with her [that's usually the case with couples who've had affairs], it would undoubtedly do tremendous damage to my family and to your reputation. But the most foolish result of all would be that I would cut myself off from you, the very source of life. So right this moment, Lord, I'm asking you to charge my battery. Thank you for letting me see this before it's too late. However long it takes, I will stay in your line until I'm free from her and filled with you." It took several months, and I had to pray this prayer many times, before I was completely free from this temptation.

Over the years a similar prayer of rejoicing has kept me, in many situations, from giving in to such temptations as envy, jealousy, fear, and anger. Rejoicing, even in times of testing, is acknowledging that *God* is the source of life. And rejoicing brings us to the place where our lives can be filled by the source of life—God himself.

Ephesians 3:14–21 contains the best explanation of rejoicing I have found:

> For this reason, I kneel before the Father, from whom his whole family in heaven and on earth derives its name. I pray that out of his glorious riches he may strengthen you with power through his Spirit in your inner being, so

that Christ may dwell in your hearts through faith. And I pray that you, being rooted and established in love, may have power, together with all the saints, to grasp how wide and long and high and deep is the love of Christ, and to know this love that surpasses knowledge—*that you may be filled to the measure of all the fullness of God.* Now to him who is able to do immeasurably more than all we ask or imagine, according to his power that is at work within us, to him be the glory in the church and in Christ Jesus throughout all generations, for ever and ever! Amen.

Note the words I italicized: *"That you may be filled to the measure of all the fullness of God."* That is God's desire for and gift to us. And in the next verse, Paul talks about him who is "able to do immeasurably more than all we ask or imagine." That's the overflow—the exciting, fulfilling life we all desire. It's waiting for us. We can experience it by rejoicing.

Rejoicing begins when we acknowledge that God is the source of all life. In fact, God *is* life, which is why we adore him and sing praises to him. Rejoicing reveals faith, because it demonstrates our expectation that God will reveal to us the depths and heights of his love. All of this is so that we may be filled up to *all* the fullness of God. That's the ultimate in fulfillment!

Make God Your Best Friend

During my time of temptation, I learned that the principle of rejoicing was reliable. Simply going to the source of joy and getting to know Jesus personally as my very best friend filled my life. Jesus wants to be our friend. Friendship with Christ is *abiding* in him. *Abiding* means depending upon his Spirit in us to guide us with a peace we feel or sense.

Here's what I do to this day. I see Christ living in me, and he alone takes the temptation of lust away through his power—not by my efforts, but by his Spirit at work in me and through me.

Obeying Jesus does not mean I am like a slave. He says in John 15:15, "I no longer call you servants, because a servant does not know his master's business. Instead, I have called you friends, for everything that I learned from my Father I have made known to you."

Most of us have enjoyed the blessings of a close friendship. When we're with that friend, we're relaxed and free to be ourselves. We enjoy each other's company. I believe that *rejoicing*—returning to each other often—is the key to fruitful friendship. That's why making God our very best friend is the way to lasting joy. To experience God's joy on a daily basis we must become God's friend.

I picture myself like the widow standing in God's line, waiting patiently for God to meet my inner spiritual needs and my material needs, as well as my family's needs. I do this while I run every morning. During the half hour to an hour that I'm pounding the pavement, I enjoy a special, uninterrupted time of building a meaningful friendship with Christ.

Each person must find the time that is right for him or her. It might be while eating or getting dressed. It might be during quiet moments of Bible reading and prayer. It might be while driving to and from work; or while ironing, cooking, or washing dishes; or during a break at work. The important thing is that we not let the cares and pressures of everyday living squeeze out our daily personal time with the One who is the *source of life*.

In addition to spending time alone with God, we must also spend time reading the Bible. Reading God's Word is essential for getting to know God's thoughts. In fact, spending time in his Word plugs us into the source of life. In John 6:63 Jesus says, "The words I have spoken to you are spirit and they are life." And in John 17:17 Jesus prays to the Father on behalf of his disciples saying, "Sanctify them by the truth; your word is truth."

There is a very important balance between *knowing* Christ and knowing *about* him. Neither worshiping the Bible nor ignoring it can bring steady spiritual growth. Reading God's Word and not developing a personal relationship with him is like reading a biography of a famous person but never meeting him and getting to know him.

But Jesus and the Word are one (John 1:1), so it is impossible to know Jesus without knowing his Word. And the only way to have an intimate friendship with him is to communicate with him, to let his words sink into our souls. Listen to the words of Jesus in John 5:39–40: "You diligently study the Scriptures because you think that by them you possess eternal life. These are the Scriptures that testify about me, yet you refuse to come to me to have life." He is LIFE—period!

I can understand this better when I think in terms of my relationship with Norma, who is my very best human friend. One of the reasons we are so close is because we have security in our relationship through consistent communication, a sharing of our deepest emotions, a communion of our spirits, and regular, meaningful touching.

That friendship with my wife didn't begin to blossom until she made God her best friend. And when I followed her example and began going to God for the meeting of my personal needs, we no longer were depending on each other to fill the lonely gaps in our lives. Relieved of those expectations, we as husband and wife were now free to become friends. There is an added benefit to marital friendship: My friendship with Norma helps me know God better as a friend.

Friendship with God is security. The apostle Paul mentions this security in Romans 8:38–39: "For I am convinced that neither death nor life, neither angels nor demons, neither the present nor the future, nor any powers, neither height nor depth, nor anything else in all creation, will be able to separate us from the love of God that is in Christ Jesus our Lord." Just as I'm committed to Norma, I'm committed to God for life, and I *know* he's committed to me.

Alcoholics Anonymous and other similar agencies have learned a powerful lesson about how to gain freedom from addictions. The key is a secure relationship with God, which seems to release God's power in us to set us free from addictions.

Friendship with God is prayer. Just as we cannot know a friend without communicating, we cannot know God without regular conversation with him through prayer. Prayer is a two-way street. I express my love, devotion, and feelings, and I listen to God as well. The closer the friendship, the more intimate our sharing. One of the reasons King David knew God so well was because he poured out his emotions in verse after verse in the psalms and contrasted his feelings with the awesome greatness of God: "How precious to me are your thoughts, O God! How vast is the sum of them! Were I to count them, they would outnumber the grains of sand. When I awake, I am still with you" (Psalm 139:17–18).

Friendship with God is identification. True friendship requires a willingness to be seen together. A person is not truly a friend unless we are willing to be identified with that person. This is one reason the sacraments of baptism and Communion are so important, and why physical signs such as kneeling, singing, and other forms of worship reflect our relationship with God.

Friendship with God is dependency. One of the benefits of knowing God as our friend is being able to express our physical and material needs to him. When we seek to know God, we are promised that our material needs will be met (Matthew 6:33), but we need to remind ourselves constantly that having our physical needs met will not give us life. Life comes only through knowing God, not from the material goods he gives us.

Friendship with God is gratefulness. An important element of a good friendship is mutual admiration, which is another way of saying we should not take each other for granted. We need to be grateful for the friendship, and sometimes we need to express our gratefulness in tangible ways.

By realizing how faithful God has been and wants to be to those who draw close to him, we can develop a grateful, thankful heart even before we receive answers to our prayers. Paul tells us in Philippians 4:6, "Do not be anxious about anything, but in everything, by prayer and petition, with thanksgiving, present your requests to God." The next verse confirms how God fills our cup. The *peace* of God, which surpasses all of our comprehension, protects our hearts and our minds in Christ Jesus.

During my time of praying about my lust, I was able to thank God for freeing me *even before* he did because I knew he would be faithful and because I knew that I would not get out of his line until he helped me. It was God's will that I be faithful to his commands and to the wife he gave me, so I was confident that he would answer my prayer for mental and physical purity.

One of the benefits of expressing gratefulness is *contentment* in knowing that God will energize my battery and provide for my needs. The same spirit that Paul describes in Philippians 4:11 has become mine, for I too have learned the secret of being content in whatever circumstances I find myself in.

Also, like the great King David, my inner experience of calm and peace continues as I follow his example in Psalm 62. My soul no longer expects anything from God's creation but waits in silence for God only. I command my soul to do the same thing David did: "Find rest, O my soul, in God alone; my hope comes from him. He alone is my rock and my salvation; he is my fortress; I will not be shaken. My salvation and my honor depend on God; he is my mighty rock, my refuge" (Psalm 62:5–7). I have determined to trust God at all times and to wait on his faithfulness.

Decide to Be Filled

The feelings associated with gratefulness and contentment may take time to develop. Contentment results from *deciding* to rest in the faithfulness of God. Calmness results from *seeing* God's faithfulness time after time. I meet many discouraged Christians who experience little of God's faithfulness because they get out of his line too soon. They don't allow God to answer in his perfect timing. Because they are discouraged, they don't feel like getting back into line. It's a defeating cycle, but we can choose to break it.

Our decision to rest in God's faithfulness can be based on the promises clearly given in Scripture. God promises to be our rock, shield, rear guard, shepherd, king, rescuer, hiding place, living water, bread of life, light, physician, and life-supplying vine; God promises to be our power to overcome sin, our advocate, our free gift of eternal life, as well as our source of wisdom, joy, peace, love, and self-control. The list goes on and on.

These promises are facts, given to God's people who stand in his line like the widow in Luke 18. Gratefulness, praise, wonder, and excitement can become real as we witness God's work in our lives. The faithful, trustworthy fact, according to the Bible, is that God provides these emotions to all who love him.

The process of discovering and knowing Jesus Christ as the source of life can continue every day for the rest of our lives. Getting to know Jesus gives life richness, for we can never fully know the depth of his love. Every day is an opportunity to see a new dimension. Unfortunately that doesn't mean we never get sidetracked or discouraged. The false promises of the world in which we live continually aim to draw us away from the source of life.

Negative emotions also draw us away from God. Anger, loneliness, and hurt feelings can make us feel as though God has deserted us or let us down. Actually, just the opposite is true. God allows these feelings to help us see where our expectations are focused—whether on God or on his creation. In the next two chapters we will find out how to use negative emotions as an early warning system, alerting us that we need to return to the source of life, which is Christ Jesus himself.

CHAPTER SIX

What Your Emotions Tell You

CHRISTIANS OUGHT TO BE the most joyful people on earth. Unfortunately, that's often not the case. Take, for example, the situation of Bob and Ellen. Both are in their second marriage, having made mistakes as young adults. For Bob, his experiences led him into a relationship with Christ; for Ellen, she has returned to the abandoned faith of her youth. The couple met at church in a Sunday school class for singles.

This couple has been married twenty-five years, but it hasn't been easy. There were two kids from Ellen's first marriage, and together they've had two more children. They have frequently argued over how to raise the kids. Ellen is often frustrated at her husband's inability to read her mind—he never seems to pick up on her hints about what he should do for her and for the house. Bob is equally frustrated, for he never seems able to please her.

This sense of tension has compounded Bob's career strug-gles. At one point he was laid off and they moved to another

wn for work. Another time he feels he was wrongly forced
out of a job. Ellen doesn't understand why he isn't more expres-
sive with his boss, or why he can't advance higher within a company. She is also envious of friends in church who have
better-paying jobs and nicer homes. While they live comfort-
ably, Ellen wonders if they will ever achieve genuine financial
security. Bob meanwhile feels like a failure, and he quietly
seethes at what he perceives to be his wife's unrelenting pressure aimed at him.

Bob and Ellen have a couple of things going for them. They
are committed to their marriage. After going through divorce,
neither wants the pain of another. And they *do* love each other.
But there is little joy in their day-to-day relationship.

Why are so many couples so unhappy? Why do we all know
Christians—those who should be plugged into the source of
joy—who have reasonably positive life circumstances, yet who
seem to be so miserable? I believe it's primarily a problem of
expectations. At one time or another all of us experience situations in which our expectations are unfulfilled, and unfulfilled
expectations are a primary cause of negative emotions and
unhappiness. Many people who struggle with negative emotions actually use them as weapons against themselves. Every
day people make statements like, "How could I have gotten so
angry at my wife?" or "I can't believe she got that raise. I know
I shouldn't feel this way, but …" or "He insists it's not personal,
but every time he says a certain thing, my feelings are hurt."

Many of us deny and try to push away these painful feelings.
But consider this:

*Anger, hurt feelings, fear, and lust can actually help
us develop a closer, more vital relationship with
Jesus Christ.*

Now on the surface that statement may sound incredible because negative emotions are usually associated with a *lack* of spiritual maturity and with unhappiness. And it's true, allowed to fester and develop, negative emotions *can* draw us away from God. We have all seen numerous examples of how the "acts of the sinful nature" (Galatians 5:19) can hurt and damage relationships. But as Christians, we need not become victims of our emotions. Even negative emotions can be the impetus that moves us back to the source of joy.

We can never completely avoid negative emotions; we will all experience anger and fear and loneliness on occasion. The issue is *how often* we have those emotions and how we use them. There are many ways to respond to negative emotions—some ways are healthy, others are not.

One unhealthy response to negative emotions is to try to stuff them deep inside or pretend they don't exist. The damage of denying our emotions is well illustrated by the story of a Spartan boy in ancient Greece. At the age of seven the boy left home to begin a lifelong career of harsh military service. He was taught every aspect of military combat. He learned survival skills and was taught to hide every trace of emotion.

One day the boy captured a fox and was playing with the animal when he saw his instructor approach him. Quickly he stuffed the wild fox underneath his cloak. In keeping with their custom, the teacher questioned the boy at length. The boy calmly responded to the teacher's endless questions, his face never betraying a hint of pain or fear even though the fox was gnawing and tearing at his unprotected body. Finally, suffering from mortal wounds, the boy fell dead at his teacher's feet. He became the model of Spartan discipline, and this story was later used as an example of genuine manhood. Yet those "manly" qualities ended up killing him.

Some Christians view such control of their emotions as a measure of spirituality. No matter how much they are struggling r hurting, they believe they must always present a facade of happiness.

The model Jesus gave us, however, was not that of a Spartan. Jesus wept at the grave of a friend. He became angry at the money changers in the temple. He was even accused of being "a glutton and a drunkard" (Matthew 11:19) because he attended weddings and other parties. Denying negative emotions may leave us looking good on the outside, but to do so will destroy us on the inside.

A second option is to allow our emotions to run their natural course with the attitude that there's nothing we can do about them. The problem with *unchecked* emotions, however, is that they can harm others as well as ourselves. Ken and Cindy are an example.

Ken came from a home where everything was always clean and neat; Cindy's family hadn't been as concerned about neatness. This difference created a great deal of conflict in their marriage. When Cindy was tired after a hard day's work, she let the housework wait for another day. This frustrated Ken, who constantly fired verbal darts at his wife: "What are these clothes doing in the corner?" "This room looks like the dust bowl." "You expect the ants to clean these dishes?"

One morning Cindy awoke to hear Ken vacuuming the living room at six o'clock. She staggered out of the bedroom and asked what he was doing. "I'm sick and tired of living in this pigpen!" he yelled. Ken's outburst of anger and his degrading comments left Cindy defeated and destroyed whatever motivation she might have had to change. But Ken seemed unaware of the damage his anger was causing his wife. Venting his negative emotions made Ken feel better for the moment, but it caused lasting scars in his relationships.

Releasing pent-up emotions may be considered good therapy in some circles, but it comes at a high price. A friend who worked at a psychiatric hospital relayed the tragic story of Brian. Brian had a great deal of anger at what he considered to

be some very unfair actions his parents had taken. As pa.
Brian's therapy he was put in a room with an inflated Bo.
doll, which was to be used as a punching bag. "Just pretend this
doll is your parents," Brian was told, "and use it to release all
your hostilities."

After destroying two BoBo dolls Brian fell to the floor in
exhaustion. His therapy was termed a success, but when he was
released from the hospital a month later he returned home and
crippled his father in a fit of rage. Neither denying nor venting
our emotions is the answer.

For Christians, another option is available:

> *Those who know Jesus Christ can use negative emotions as warning signals.*

Ken looked at Cindy as the *cause* of his anger, not realizing
that his anger actually revealed a problem within him. If Ken
had been willing, he could have harnessed the power of his
anger to draw him closer to God—even to make him more loving. How is this possible? If we recognize that negative emotions are like warnings on a computer screen, we can use them
to warn us that we are headed for trouble.

Emotions Provide Important Information

Computers today routinely send us messages about the condition
of the software and hardware. Recently I was working on-line
when suddenly this message appeared on the screen: "Your program has performed an illegal operation and will shut down."
Before I could respond, my America Online connection was sev-
ered, and I was left scratching my head, wondering, *What did I do
wrong?* A moment later, I logged back on to AOL and resumed

work. I never learned what criminal act my computer managed to foist on my behalf.

That incident was a rather minor inconvenience. Others have genuine horror stories because they failed to carefully read an on-screen warning. A friend of mine, Larry, isn't very comfortable with computers, though he has to use one in his job. Several years ago, he typed in a command to erase a file. As usual, the computer asked if he was sure. Without carefully reading the message, Larry pushed "Y," then was horrified as he read the message, "Deleting All Files." A major project for work was lost, and though he had some of the material on backup disks, it took him more than a week to recover and repair the project. It also took about that long for his heart to calm down to its usual pace.

Since then, Larry has been paranoid about computer error messages. He now works on a network system at work and sometimes gets messages about the network server. The company help desk often gets panicked calls from Larry, and they have to reassure him, "Don't worry. You'll be off-line for a half hour. You didn't do anything wrong. You won't lose any data."

For a couple of years, Larry used a temperamental laptop computer. Occasionally, the screen locked up while the computer rang a loud warning bell. It was on that machine that he saw his first "fatal error" message. It read, "A fatal error has occurred and this program will shut down in 60 seconds." There was a little "OK" box he was supposed to click to acknowledge the message, but all Larry could do was sit in front of the screen, afraid to touch the machine, while the bell continued its maddening harangue.

For many couples, emotions are about as helpful as computer error messages. Yet, for a technical expert, these computer screen messages reveal a lot of information. When Larry talks to the help desk, the support person often asks Larry to read him the message, including any code numbers. Then she calmly tells

Larry what it means and walks him through the process of _____ ing the problem. It may mean adjusting a setting on a program then restarting the machine. She stays on the phone until Larry has completed all the steps and is successfully working again.

Larry has another option when error messages come on his computer. He can punch buttons and smack the computer screen, telling it to shape up. (In fact, he used that approach a few times with his temperamental laptop.) Of course, that approach ultimately does no good. Larry can also ignore a warning and try to continue what he's doing on the computer. Sometimes that even works, for a while. But if the problem isn't addressed, he can be sure the message will reappear.

In my counseling, I regularly see people handling emotions without any idea of their meaning. They come to me with error messages screaming in their lives, but instead of using the valuable information the messages could provide them, they ignore them or try to smash them.

Emotions tell us what cord we're using. If you are experiencing genuine love, peace, and joy (the fruit of the Spirit), you know you are connected to God's 220-volt power source. If you continually have emotions like envy, jealousy, worry, fear, or anger, you know you're trying to be charged by a 110-volt power source, and you know that this ultimately won't work. Negative emotions should remind you to change extension cords and plug again into the source of joy, which is God through Jesus Christ.

Probably the most important thing that negative emotions reveal is our misguided expectations. This is a critical point: *Expectations determine emotions.* If we can understand and control our expectations from the world—from people, things, and work—our emotions will naturally follow.

Let's examine seven common emotions—looking at three in this chapter and four in the next—and see what they reveal about our expectations; then let's explore how each emotion can be used to draw us to a closer walk with God. In the process, will see how our negative emotions can lead us back to the source of our fulfillment.

Envy—Desire for Gain

Envy is the desire to gain what appears to make others happy—a bigger home, a better car, a higher-paying job. We think that having these things will finally make us content.

Perhaps we keep our eyes on Jesus most of the day, knowing that he alone fulfills us, but in quiet moments early in the morning, during a coffee break, or on the drive to and from work, the green cloud of envy settles over us and we wish we had more of what the Joneses have. They appear to be so happy. Of course, if we lived with them for a few weeks, we might discover that they are just good actors. Behind their closed doors, Mr. and Mrs. Jones may be wishing they had what we have.

I rarely experience envy anymore. But for many years it often engulfed me, especially when I traveled with members of Bill Gothard's management team. One time, I accidentally learned that one of my subordinates was making a significantly higher salary than I was, even though he had far less experience in the ministry. For several days and nights I felt envy and anger because of that inequity. I formulated several plans to reveal the injustice without sounding like I was complaining. But Bill discovered the mistake about the same time I did and doubled my salary before I even had a chance to talk to him. It had been an innocent oversight. Bill was so immersed in his cause that he rarely thought about financial rewards for himself or others in the organization. But doubling my salary did not eliminate my envy, because I could always find someone else who made more money and owned more things. I came to realize that money and possessions would never energize me. The only good my envy served was to remind me that *God alone is my source of life.*

The reason I seldom feel envy anymore is because I know that nothing others possess can permanently satisfy. When I do

feel envy, I pray, "Lord, thank you for this emotion. Help
see that what I want can never fill me up as much as you can. I
fact, looking for happiness in your creation is like idol worship
in your eyes. I'm glad you honor those who turn from idols to
worship you" (based on 1 Thessalonians 1:9).

The next emotion is closely related to envy.

Jealousy—Fear of Loss

Whereas envy is wanting something we don't have, jealousy is the
fear of losing what we already possess.

Jealousy is what we feel when someone flirts with our mate,
when a special friend moves away, or when our position at
work is threatened.

In high school, I dated Susan fairly steadily for nearly three
years. During our senior year she went to California for a vacation, and when she returned she informed me she had met
another guy. Those next few days I was miserably jealous. I lost
ten pounds. I couldn't concentrate on my after-school job, and
my boss finally told me either to quit or to make up with my
girlfriend.

After the boss's ultimatum, I left work early and went over
to Susan's house. When I told her how miserable I was, she
broke down and cried. What a thrill it was to have her back. But
the excitement didn't last very long. Within a month, we were
having major problems. I was constantly questioning the relationship. I was never sure she wouldn't leave me again. Instead
of being able to relax and enjoy her company, my fear of losing
her a second time drove away all my positive feelings and made
me suspicious of any other guy who talked to her.

Although I didn't realize it at the time, I can see now that my
jealousy actually revealed my own selfishness. My unspoken
expectation was to establish control of the relationship and of
her. If we were going to break up again, I wanted to be the one
to do it, not her.

Negative emotions reveal to us that we are viewing the world as if its only purpose is to satisfy *our* needs. When we expect individuals and things to cooperate with our specially designed program to bring us satisfaction, it's not surprising that we get envious and jealous when those goals are frustrated, delayed, or postponed.

As with envy, to counteract jealousy I approach the Lord in prayer: "Lord, I'm afraid of losing something that I already have. However, I want my treasure to be with you in heaven, not here. I realize that whatever I have that I enjoy can never permanently charge my battery. Even if I lose something I need, I can come to you, the giver of life, and ask for another. And if you don't want me to have it, I can ask you to take away the desire. Thank you that *you*, not my possessions, are the source of life."

Some men fear losing their wife because it would end their best friendship as well as take away their sexual outlet. They fail to remember that God is strong enough to handle every need. Andre Thornton, a former major league baseball player whose wife was killed in a tragic car accident, understands this truth. Andre honestly faced his emotions through prayer:

> I asked God to quench my sex drive, even though since the accident I hadn't felt any sexual feelings whatsoever. But I knew myself well enough to know that someday those desires would return. I knew the temptations that came to professional athletes. I knew the women who hung around baseball teams. There would be opportunities on road trips to get into compromising situations, and I didn't want to do anything to disgrace the name of Christ. So I asked God to kill any sexual desires until he brought along someone to take Gert's place in my life. God was faithful in answering this prayer too.[1]

---

[1]Andre Thornton, quoted by Al Janssen, *Triumph Born of Tragedy* (Eugene, Ore.: Harvest House, 1983), 105.

Some people have a hard time admitting that jealousy i̇ error message in their lives. Letting it stay on-screen for to long can cause major problems. Spouses, children, and possessions are simply on loan to us from the Lord. We do not own them. Continually fearing the loss of a person or a possession can end in emotional and spiritual defeat.

The next emotion is probably one of the most destructive desires drawing men and women away from God. It lurks behind every marriage, seeking to sink its talons into an unprepared victim. At almost every men's retreat I teach I am asked to address this subject. At conferences for pro athletes, when we have a question-and-answer time for men only, this topic always comes up first.

Lust—Dreaming About What I Can't or Shouldn't Have

Lust makes us think that having some person we don't presently have would make us happier. Often that person is simply a figment of our imagination. Even if the person is real, we often attach character traits to him or her that are not real. Usually our lust focuses on sexual involvement. We imagine someone who is terribly fond of us and who prefers our presence and intimacy over anyone else's. We imagine that if we had such a person to hold in our arms, it would be exciting and wonderfully fulfilling. This is a terrible deception, for we forget or ignore the devastating consequences of living out our imaginations.

Sensual imaginations reveal our selfish desire for stimulation. Unchecked, sensual stimulation actually increases the desire. We see this exhibited in several ways. For example, one of the primary reasons people smoke or consume alcohol or drugs is to stimulate their physical senses. As a person continues in this selfish frame of mind, the desire grows until he or she needs regular and increasing doses of stimulation.

Psychiatrist Gerald May observes that God created us to "attach" to him. All humans have a God-given, built-in need to

.ch to God in a meaningful way. When we ignore God, we .stead try to attach to his creation—people, things, and career. This is where all types of addictions are formed.[2]

Even if we feel we've conquered lust, the emotion can strike when we least expect it. One friend discovered this when he spoke at a Christian conference. Dick's wife was in the final months of pregnancy, so they were not as sexually active as usual. While several hundred miles away from home, Dick suddenly found himself infatuated with a woman attending the conference. She was attractive and seemed to enjoy his company. But while admitting his normal sexual drive was heating up, he also knew that yielding to that desire would bring at best only a very temporary satisfaction. He came face-to-face with his own selfish desire to be stimulated and realized that the devastating long-term consequences to his ministry, to his wife and kids, and to his relationship with God would far outweigh any momentary pleasure. That knowledge helped him control his physical drive, which took about forty-eight hours to subside.

The motivation behind extramarital affairs seems to be very different for men and women. Men tend to lust for physical release or conquest, viewing women as challenges for satisfying their sexual drives. Women, on the other hand, tend to involve themselves in affairs because of their deep need for communication and a meaningful relationship—a deep need that is not being met.

Recently we've seen a huge increase in affairs on the Internet. These affairs don't need to be consummated to cause a serious threat to a marriage. Many women find themselves more comfortable talking with a stranger in a chat room than to their own husbands. Many men enjoy the power they seem to have counseling a woman by means of an impersonal computer

---

[2]See Gerald May, *Addiction and Grace: Love and Spirituality in the Healing of Addictions* (New York: HarperCollins, 1991), 1–20, 91–118.

rather than face-to-face. In too many cases, men and women let their imaginations go wild in these relationships.

How can we use lust to strengthen our relationship with God? First, by recognizing the basic motive behind this emotion. Lust is not serving a person in love; it is viewing a person as an object to be used. This happens even within the marriage relationship. With Norma, I had to realize that I was violating God's law by trying to use her for my own happiness rather than loving her by serving her needs.

Second, lust can reconfirm our awareness that God—not another's body, not even our mate's—is the source of our fulfillment. As pleasurable as sex can be, it can never substitute for the lasting joy and satisfaction of knowing God.

Third, in the midst of lustful thoughts, as an act of our will, we can pray something like this: "Lord, I know there are times when I wish my mate acted sexier. And there are even times I have entertained thoughts about being in the arms of another person. All the advertisements on TV have tried to convince me it would be exciting. But right here and now I continue to trust you to energize my life and provide all I need. I am willing to rest and wait in your faithfulness. I don't even know all I'm trying to gain from these lustful thoughts, but you know, and I know you'll meet my needs as you always have."

Because God knows our thoughts, we can share them with him and admit that we don't understand. That's what Paul instructs us to do in Romans: "[God's] Spirit helps us in our weakness. We do not know what we ought to pray for, but … he who searches our hearts knows the mind of the Spirit, because the Spirit intercedes for the saints in accordance with God's will" (Romans 8:26–27).

What practical help can we offer those stuck in the quicksand of lustful desire? Some try to struggle out of the grip it has on their lives through visualization, masturbation, or regular participation in sexual activity. But the more we struggle, the deeper we sink. If no one is available to pull us out, the one way to escape from quicksand is to relax, lie back in the sand, take a deep breath, fill your lungs with air, and allow your limbs to float to the top. We can take similar action with lust by not fighting our thoughts and desires and instead ask Jesus to perform what he promises to do—release us from bondage. He can supernaturally pull us out as we rest in him.

If no one is available to pull you out of quicksand, you can still escape by slowly moving your arms above your head, putting them slightly into the sand, and swimming slowly to the edge, as if doing a slow-motion backstroke. Experts say it may take several hours to swim just a few feet. But freedom is as close as the bank. When battling lust, we can do the same thing by persistently *looking to Jesus* for strength and patience.

I have known men stuck in the mire of lust who didn't make it to freedom for several months. It may take a year or more for some to "swim" to freedom. Day after day we must reconfirm truths given to us by Jesus. God promises he is faithful to answer the requests of his children. "Therefore I tell you, whatever you ask for in prayer, believe that you have received it, and it will be yours" (Mark 11:24). And, "If you remain in me and my words remain in you, ask whatever you wish, and it will be given you" (John 15:7). Real freedom comes from abiding in a close relationship with God and from allowing God's Word to become alive in us. The Bible urges us to "live a life of love.... But among you there must not be even a *hint* of sexual immorality" (Ephesians 5:2–3, italics added). And, "It is for freedom that Christ has set us free. Stand firm, then, and do not let yourselves be burdened again by a yoke of slavery" (Galatians 5:1). It is God's will that we experience freedom from lust, so we can stand in his line daily, knowing it is just a matter of time before he will bring us freedom from sexual slavery.

Once we're free from the quicksand, we're usually weak from the effort. Here are four ways to regain strength and remain strong so we don't fall back into the mire.

First, rehearse the negative consequences of sexual involvement, even in the midst of lustful thoughts. Remember what it feels like to be trapped. The consequences are far more than we can mention here, but they include enslavement to passion (see Galatians 5:1); reinforcement of our self-centered tendency that diminishes genuine expression of love; callousness of our soul (see Ephesians 4:19); and, of course, the possibility of catching a sexual disease. In other words, the truth and life of God are darkened within us when we engage in unrighteousness (see Romans 1:18–32).

Second, memorize sections of Scripture that deal specifically with sexual freedom. After memorizing them, persistently ask God to make your life consistent with these verses. Start with Galatians 5:1–14, Ephesians 5:1–6, and 1 Thessalonians 4:3–7.

Remember, when we read God's Word, we don't read it for what we can do by our own efforts. Don't think, "I need to start living more by this or that law." Rather, read God's Word and see his commandments as what *you'll look like* as you continue to abide in Christ. "If you love me, you will obey what I command," the Lord says (John 14:15). Keep your focus on loving, knowing, and abiding in him—and watch *him* enrich and strengthen your life.

Third, for men especially, beware of the anger/lust cycle that often develops. Many men experience their most severe times of lust after a struggle or problem at home or at work. If we fail to make things right after a disagreement or confrontation, we may be setting ourselves up for temptation, because such encounters leave us feeling depressed and inadequate. Because none of us likes to feel bad about ourselves, we look for something to perk us up, to make us feel powerful and important again.

Sexual stimulation can have a temporary euphoric effect. Like alcohol or drugs, it can bring about a heightened sense of self-worth—until the shame and reality of our actions bring us crashing down. Some men who never take a drink or try drugs submit to a life of erotic escapades that is every bit as addictive—and deadly. Sin always takes you further down the path of destruction than you want to go.

Writing in the book of Proverbs, Solomon has sobering words for those who use any form of lust—actual sexual encounters, fantasy, or pornographic pictures—to make up for feelings of anger or low self-worth: "For the lips of an adulteress drip honey, and her speech is smoother than oil; but in the end she is bitter as gall, sharp as a double-edged sword" (Proverbs 5:3–4).

Giving in to lust does not break the anger/lust cycle; it only intensifies it. Now we are not only angry and depressed about our problem at work or at home, but we are also angry about our lack of self-control. And on top of our shame, those of us who are Christians also have the Holy Spirit convicting us of sin.

Genuine repentance is a biblical solution, but getting furious with ourselves and vowing it will never happen again do little good. In fact, when we browbeat ourselves (a way of punishing ourselves so that God won't, or so that he will "let us off the hook"), we actually dig a deeper rut for ourselves and set ourselves up for our next "lust fix."

Unless we truthfully deal with the anger/lust cycle and admit it is signaling that a relationship needs repair or that we need the help of a Christian friend or counselor, we may continue in the downward spiral for years. This vicious circle of sin can cause even Christians to spin so fast that right seems wrong and wrong seems right. But returning to Christ's healing is always the answer.

Finally, realize that for most people the gaining of freedom from lust is a long-term process, especially for those who have developed a habit of immoral thoughts and actions. You might consider starting or joining a support group for those who struggle in this area. This can be a men-only or women-only group, who testify as to how God has produced freedom and who encourage and support one another in memorizing and meditating on Scripture. These folks also hold each other accountable, pray with each other, and talk honestly about their entrapment. Much healing can come just by confessing our weakness and praying for each other: "Therefore confess your sins to each other and pray for each other so that you may be healed. The prayer of a righteous man is powerful and effective" (James 5:16).

Al meets regularly with several other men in a discipleship group. Once he returned from a business trip and reported that his hotel room had a cable movie station. He watched a PG-rated movie, then started to watch a sexually explicit film but caught himself and turned it off. However, he expressed concern about handling temptation on an upcoming ten-day trip. One of the members asked Al to develop a plan for using any of the time that was not being spent in meetings, which he did.

On his return Al had to give a report. Near the end of the trip he had found himself seated next to a single woman at an athletic event. The thought entered his mind, "You could take her out for dinner and no one would ever know." Rather than allow time to entertain the thought any further, he left the game early. *Knowing he was accountable to men back home helped him resist temptation* because he knew they would ask him how he did. Accountability is good, but remember that it doesn't replace the most important solution—God's grace doing its work in us.

I have focused on the sexual aspects of lust because it is so out-of-control in our society. But other forms of lust—such as craving sweets, overeating, and stimulating the senses through drugs and alcohol—can be just as damaging. The thoughts I've shared can apply in any area of sensual temptation that robs us of life.

What error messages appear most frequently in your life? Jealousy, envy, or lust? Take the time necessary to deal with those emotions.

CHAPTER SEVEN

Overcoming Emotions
That Destroy Joy

HAVE YOU EVER WALKED confidently out on a long limb only to look back and see someone sawing it from the tree? That's how I felt recently when I realized what I'd done to Norma.

It was really an innocent mistake. We'd been living for several years in Branson, Missouri, but we still had a couple of bank accounts in Phoenix, where we used to live. Logically, I thought it would be good to combine everything into one bank, so I closed out the accounts in Phoenix and invested the money in a fund I had at our local bank.

A couple of years later, our accountant asked me about a bank account in Phoenix. "Oh, we closed that a couple of years ago," I told him.

"Then why is there still activity in there?" he asked. He told me the amount of money.

I thought that was strange, so I asked Norma about it. She revealed that this was a special savings account she had set up. Each month she put a little of her paycheck in the account, which she uses for our children and grandchildren. Sudden realized that she didn't know I had "closed out" the accou because she had kept making deposits.

I explained this to my accountant, who then wanted to know what had happened to the money I'd withdrawn. "I reinvested it," I explained.

My accountant was a wise man who had learned some things about marriage from my seminar. "Gary, I think we should go together and explain this to Norma."

So we told Norma the situation. She frowned for a moment and said, "Well, I wondered why that account was so low. Now I know who stole it!"

"No, no, I just reinvested it!" I tried to explain. Then she laughed and kidded us some more about it. I breathed a sigh of relief. She didn't seem mad. Everything was okay.

But everything wasn't okay. Periodically, she would say something like, "I'm never going to trust you again with any of my personal funds," or "I can't believe you stole my money." It was said somewhat lightheartedly, so it took me nearly two years before I realized that something was bothering her—and I wasn't getting it. So finally, I asked Norma why she kept referring to this incident.

Norma explained: "Gary, you don't understand that you and Dan stole my money, and you haven't given it back."

"We haven't stolen it," I protested. "We simply reinvested it. It's your money. If you want it, take it."

"No, you don't understand. I don't know what account that money is in, and so I don't have access to it. It's not in my name."

"Oh, I see. Then what do I need to do to repair this situation?" I asked.

"I need you to go to the bank, get a cashier's check for that amount—with interest—and give it to me so I can do what I want to with it. After all, it's my money."

Okay, I'll do it." And I did. Honestly, I didn't understand why it was such a big deal until I asked a few other women. They all understood exactly what Norma was saying. Even though it didn't seem like a big deal to me, I needed to make things right because it was important to Norma.

This example illustrates how a husband and wife can have their feelings hurt. Left to fester, this situation could have divided Norma and me; in fact, in many marriages it's events like this—often simple misunderstandings—that have catastrophic consequences because of how people choose to process them.

It all has to do with how others respond to our goals. These goals may be verbalized, but often they are unspoken expectations that the mate never discovers. In this chapter we'll look at four more emotions. Of the four, one is the most damaging to a marriage. In fact, it is the number one cause of marital unhappiness. It can rob a couple of most or all of their energy. It's the cause of most conflicts. And uncorrected, it often leads to divorce.

But before we go there, let's look at three other emotions that, unresolved, lead to this devastating last emotion.

Hurt Feelings—No One Appreciates My Goals

Early in our marriage, I served a church as an assistant pastor. In my second year, I was feeling rather confident of my ability and accomplishments, so at a council meeting, I proposed that the church purchase a bus for the youth program.

My recommendations for what I thought was an obvious need were met with harsh criticism. One council member after another began to make comments and ask questions like, "Why don't you run the youth group like it's been run in previous years?" "You should slow down and not make so many changes." "Did you think your ways are superior? We've been doing things the same way for fifteen years. Why are we suddenly wrong when you came on board?"

The sudden and intense criticism stunned me, and I w̶
offended that no one on my committee supported me, not eve̶
the pastor. I thought to myself, "They don't pay me enough to
take this kind of abuse. Why am I subjecting myself to this?
Somewhere there must be a church where people will appreciate my talents. It's obvious this congregation doesn't want me."

I slithered home that night and woke up Norma to pour out
my woes. I complained about how I'd been mistreated and suggested that I ought to quit. She tried to encourage me.

Unable to sleep, I sat in the kitchen and pondered my situation. I reached for my Bible but didn't feel like reading it. On
the scratch pad by the phone I wrote, "Why do people in the
church continue to hurt my feelings? Why do they make me so
angry?" "Lord," I pleaded, "show me what I can do for these
poor people. How can I penetrate the hardness of their hearts?
What would it take to break through their stubborn resistance
and help them see your love?" If necessary, I was willing to stay
up all night and read every chapter of the Bible to find help. I
was tired of having my emotions manipulated by members of
the church.

For several hours, I could not figure out what to do to help
those people. It never occurred to me that my conflict with the
church might be *my* fault, that *I* might need to change or adjust
some attitudes and actions. I could only think that if *they* were
more supportive, more committed to Christ, more dedicated, then
I'd be happy. If they'd only step out of the past and start implementing my fresh ideas, I wouldn't be having these problems.

Sound familiar? No wonder Jesus said in Matthew 7:3:
"Why do you look at the speck of sawdust in your brother's eye
and pay no attention to the plank in your own eye?"

Sometime early the next morning, light began to dawn in my
mind and I caught a glimpse of the plank in my own eye: I
wasn't *serving* these people; I had unconsciously tried to *use*
them for my own self-centered goals. In seminary I had learned

many creative ways to run a church education program. implementing those ideas became my goal for this church. Though I never verbalized it, I expected the pastor, the Sunday school committee, and the church membership to follow my lead without question. Couldn't they recognize the genius of my fresh, creative ideas? I interpreted their negative response to my many new ideas as a personal rejection of me.

When church members did not cooperate with my personal goals, I got hurt feelings. But how could they possibly cooperate if they didn't know my goals? I had never shared them—to do so would have exposed my self-centeredness. I had forgotten what a genuine minister is—one who *serves* the needs of those around him. No wonder the church reacted against me. I had never bothered to find out *their* goals. I had hurt *their* feelings because I had changed their programs, and they had hurt *my* feelings because they did not cooperate with my unstated goals.

UNDERSTANDING AND USING HURT FEELINGS

Hurt feelings are closely connected with anger but are slightly different. Unchecked, they can lead to anger, then bitterness, and even depression. Hurt feelings are those frustrating emotions that emerge from the unexpected. They let us know we are trying to use someone for our own benefit who is not cooperating with us.

Usually when our feelings are hurt it's because we had hoped that the offending individual would make us happy in some way. We may have expected the person to say or do something that we planned to use for our own fulfillment. When the person didn't cooperate, we may have responded with tears, pouting, an angry reaction, or a quiet disappointment, hoping that our reaction might provoke the person to change and treat us in the way we first expected them to. If the person refused to change, we may have tried the silent treatment for two or three days. We may have been tempted to get even or to run to someone else for sympathy.

ESCAPING THE PAIN OF HURT FEELINGS

That night after my disastrous church council meeting, the first thing I had to do was *admit* my problem. With deep conviction I confessed: "Lord, I never realized until now the fuller meaning of what a real servant is." Somehow I had forgotten that the second most important commandment God gave us is to love one another. I had misrepresented myself as a minister, especially as an assistant pastor. To my shame, I hadn't even taken the time to ask the one I was assisting what direction he wanted to go. Where did the pastor want to take the church? What did *he* feel was important? What would *he* like me to do? My primary objective had been to design my own program and to find ways to get everyone, including the pastor, to follow it. Did I only want a successful program that would reflect my talent and lead me to bigger and better positions?

I never did get to sleep that night, and I could hardly wait to get to church in the morning. When I arrived, I immediately called the pastor to ask if I could see him. When he invited me into his office, I confessed, "Pastor, that meeting was rough last night. But it showed me something very important. Early this morning I realized that I have been violating a major biblical principle. For two years I have tried to get everyone in this church to follow my program, my goals, my vision. It honestly never occurred to me, as your assistant, to ask *you* where God is leading you to take this church."

"After the meeting last night, I thought the reason you wanted to see me was to resign," he said with a smile.

I asked him to forgive me for my poor example as a minister and as his assistant. Then I asked him to share with me his goals and how I might assist him in reaching them. I wanted to learn how to use all my resources and training to help him, the church council, the youth sponsors, and the members of the church to reach their own spiritual goals.

That was the turning point in our relationship. He not only forgave me, but he immediately started treating me like a son. He still got frustrated with me occasionally, but instead of allowing my feelings to be hurt I would ask what I could do to help remove any roadblocks from his ministry or how I could encourage him or comfort him.

Obviously, this is a lesson I've had to learn over and over. And marriage seems like the most common source for the experience of hurt feelings. While we were living in Phoenix, Norma and I attended a dinner party. During a discussion about the quality of life in Phoenix, I proudly announced that it's like paradise. In the winter you can have a fire in your fireplace almost every night and still swim in an outdoor pool during the day.

When someone asked how cold it actually gets in the winter, I quipped, "It can drop into the low 20s."

Norma laughed and said, "That shows how observant he is," and she went right on talking.

I didn't hear anything else she said that evening. My feelings were hurt. I couldn't understand why she would make such a belittling statement and embarrass me in front of all those people. Besides, I was sure I knew how cold it gets in Phoenix. I was tempted to ask the hosts if they had an encyclopedia. I wanted to prove I wasn't stupid!

It bothered me so much that I didn't speak to Norma on the way home. When she asked if anything was wrong, I snapped, "No!" I had a cauldron full of emotions churning within me. I was ashamed for feeling so hurt, yet angry that she would be so insensitive. When I finally mentioned the problem, she apologized and said she hadn't meant the statement to come out that way. Yet I remembered her words and still felt irritated.

Before I fell asleep, I prayed, "Lord, as hard as it is to express these words, thank you that my feelings were hurt tonight. This 'error message' helps me see again my own self-centered tendencies. What those people think of me does not matter because their opinions have nothing to do with my self-worth. Only your opinion matters. Norma didn't mean to hurt my feelings, and my reaction to her comments reveals that I have tried to charge my battery with the wrong power source—other people's opinions. I expected Norma to say things to make me look intelligent. I guess that shows how quickly we can drift from you. Before I fall asleep, I want to thank you that I can look to you for my fulfillment rather than to Norma or anyone else." My hurt lasted only a few more minutes and was gone by the time I drifted off to sleep.

Even when someone deliberately tries to hurt our feelings we can still apply this principle. We don't have to allow hurt feelings to defeat us.

Fear and Worry—What If I Can't Achieve My Goals

One weekend my lawyer told me I needed to call him first thing Monday morning because he had received correspondence from the Internal Revenue Service. For hours over the next two days I worried, imagining all kinds of horrible scenarios—getting audited, owing thousands of dollars, learning I wasn't doing what I should be doing, getting a lien slapped on my house. On and on the thoughts persisted.

To make matters worse, I couldn't reach my lawyer on Monday! When I finally talked to him on Tuesday afternoon, I learned he couldn't make a corporate decision about my ministry without knowing if I intended to change the name of the organization. It was a minor question, certainly not worth spending any time worrying about. That same day I received a letter from him saying he had thoroughly checked out our finances with my accountant and everything was in order. How typical. We often waste valuable energy worrying about something that turns out to be insignificant.

How many of us pass through a day without experiencing one or both of these emotions? Either fretting about the implications of some action or dreading what may happen in the future is common, but not healthy. All of us are familiar with that gnawing, sickening feeling that eats at our insides when the promotion we expected and needed in order to meet our financial obligations is in jeopardy; when something we treasure is in danger of being lost; when we are given an ultimatum—accept a transfer to a strange city or look for another job—or when a person we respect has lost confidence in us.

Fear reveals our attitude toward personal loss. The greater the loss, the greater the fear. Worry, a form of fear, is preoccupation with the possibility that we may lose something valuable.

Fear or worry often affects communication within marriage. Often men bottle up their anxious and fearful thoughts, never telling their wives what's going on and often causing the women to worry about the stability of their relationship. Al remembers the time he had a conflict with his boss. For two days, the issue consumed him. When his wife asked him what was wrong, he avoided speaking about the problem. She prayed for him without knowing the specific issue.

Finally, Al took action and confronted his boss with certain facts. They talked and resolved the problem. That evening, Jo noticed her husband's relaxed face. During their walk, he explained the whole situation. "Why didn't you just tell me?" she wanted to know. It would have saved her so much anxiety if she could simply have understood what was going on.

REASONS FOR FEAR AND WORRY

Whenever Norma or I begin to feel fear or worry, we thank God for the feeling, then test the following six reasons until we understand the source. Simply identifying the reason for our worry often calms our anxiety. I remember these six areas by trying to pronounce a word spelled FRMPTH (sounds like *from the*):

Future—Am I (or we) worried about something in our future? For a couple, it might be finding a better-paying job or finding the down payment for a first home. Some might worry about earning enough money to provide for their children's education. Someone whose spouse is sick might be anxious about having enough money to pay the bills. Whatever it is, recognize that those things are *not* the source of joy.

Reputation—Am I worried that my reputation will be smeared? Sometimes I fear being on television because I'm afraid I will say something to embarrass myself or my family or God. If that's the basis for my worry, I take the simple steps we'll discuss in chapter 9 and the anxiety disappears almost immediately.

Money—Am I worried about losing money or not earning enough money? Norma and I remind ourselves that money does not provide fulfillment. God can bring me, like he brought the apostle Paul, to the place where I am content whether I have much or whether I have little (see Philippians 4:10–18).

Possessions—Am I worried about losing or not gaining possessions? I identify the items and then remember Jim Elliot's statement: "He is no fool who gives what he cannot keep to gain what he cannot lose."

Time—Am I worried about not having enough time? I ask myself the following questions: "Is someone misusing my time?" (If we don't set our own schedules, someone else is likely to do it for us.) "Am I procrastinating?" "Am I up against an impossible writing deadline?" I remind myself that God controls time and that he has given me enough to accomplish all he wants me to do. So I resolve to use wisely what God gives me and to respond to each interruption as though it came from God. Even if worry about unmet deadlines awakens me in the middle of the night, I need not worry about not getting enough sleep. Instead I can use the time for fellowship with God, which in itself is gain. With the Lord, tomorrow's loss or gain cannot affect my fulfillment. So I can relax and even enjoy my insomnia. Usually that helps me fall asleep.

Health—Am I worried about losing my health or my spouse losing her health? Do I get discouraged when I find more wrinkles and gray hairs? Do I worry about my weight? On these occasions I remind myself that my health is in God's hands and that even poor health cannot keep me from experiencing a fulfilling life. When I was in seminary I worried about my reputation, which caused my stomach to churn, which made me worry about getting an ulcer, which made me worry that people would discover I was not at peace with God, which would ruin my reputation! Of all people, how could a minister not be at peace with God? Now, however, I know that having people think well of me offers only temporary satisfaction at best. I still need to remind myself often of the futility of trying to convince others of my spiritual value.

One way to counteract the fear and worry associated with any of the above causes is to recall memorized Scripture. For example, meditating on portions of Psalm 37, 62, or 103 helps put problems in perspective. Think about the meaning of phrases such as "Do not fret because of evil men" (Psalm 37:1); "Delight yourself in the LORD" (Psalm 37:4); "Better the little that the righteous have than the wealth of many wicked" (Psalm 37:16); "If the LORD delights in a man's way, he makes his steps firm; though he stumble, he will not fall, for the LORD upholds him with his hand" (Psalm 37:23–24); "[The LORD] is my rock and my salvation; he is my fortress, I will never be shaken" (Psalm 62:2); and "God is our refuge" (Psalm 62:8).

Lately Norma and I have noticed an interesting development regarding our weight. After Norma gave birth to our second child, she found it impossible to get back to what she weighed at the time of our marriage. This can be a rather common problem for women, but for a long time, I didn't understand. I wanted Norma to maintain the same figure she had when we first met. What made it more difficult for her was that I had never had a weight problem. That is, I didn't—until about four years ago. Suddenly I gained a few pounds and couldn't lose them. Norma and I ended up going to Weight Watchers together, something I'd never thought would happen to me.

Looking back, I realize Norma had a lot of anxiety about her appearance, and I didn't appreciate it; in fact, I fueled that anxiety. Now that I have gained ten pounds, I've become anxious about *my* appearance. I've had to get in line and pray. I thank God for how he created me, and I thank him for the beautiful wife he has given me. I acknowledge that our appearance is not the source of my joy—*God* is. And I have tried to honor my wife as she is, with her many fantastic qualities, and to accept the fact that I am getting older and my body is changing.

Recently, after I had prayed for God to give me the energy to lose weight, he did it in one day. I waited for about a month, praying each day for him to act and give me the victory. Then someone handed me a book about eating God's way, and, miraculously, the desire to eat properly came inside me.[1] I've lost the weight, and I'm feeling great!

It seems like the longer we live, the more opportunities we have to turn negative emotions into opportunities to experience joy. What makes negative emotions like worry and fear exciting is that we can deal with them as error messages and move on to lead productive lives. These emotions don't have to defeat us when we understand the One to whom they point us.

Loneliness—No One Shares My Goal

From the moment of birth we need other people. Marriage is so important because it is one of God's primary methods of meeting this need. Yet our need for relationship can be a double-edged

---

[1] The book referred to is Rex Russell, *What the Bible Says About Healthy Living: Three Biblical Principles That Will Change Your Diet and Improve Your Health* (Ventura, Calif.: Regal, 1996).

sword. The fulfillment we find in relationships is sharply contrasted to the feelings of emptiness when we are alone.

God himself is a God of relationships. In the beginning, God said, "Let *us* make man in *our* image" (Genesis 1:26, italics added). The Father, Son, and Holy Spirit mirror our need to be in relationship to others and explain the emptiness and frustration we feel when we are alone.

Perhaps one reason the Lord provided us with a "family of believers" is so we would always have spiritual mothers, fathers, sisters, and brothers to love us (see 1 Timothy 5). A loving church can be a haven for lonely people.

Yet for some people, the loneliness they feel is not based on a lack of people in their lives, but on their own selfish actions or desires. Jim's wife, Betty, had just given birth to their second child in less than two years. With all of the demands on Betty's time, Jim began to feel left out and unwanted. He turned to a secretary at work to boost his self-worth, and in almost no time they were having an affair.

Jim set out to relieve his feelings of loneliness in a sinful way, and he only compounded his pain. Today, four years later, his wife and children live in another state, and the other woman is living with another man. For Jim, the pain keeps driving his loneliness deeper and deeper—and may in fact do so for years to come.

Although Jim's example is extreme, loneliness can be a symptom of a selfish desire to control another's time or affection—even if it is not best for them or others.

When the birth of Michael, our third child, required me to cut back on travel, I often shuttled the travel team back and forth from the office to the airport. After dropping them off I'd feel lonely as I recalled their parting statements: "We'll miss you in Minneapolis"; "We'll say 'hi' to all your friends in Seattle"; or "We'll bring you some bread from San Francisco." I'd drive back to an empty office, sometimes feeling resentment toward

Michael for what he was denying me. I had to learn it was only *Jesus Christ,* not those trips or the camaraderie of my colleagues, who could give me lasting fulfillment. The loneliness I felt was selfish, not genuine. Once I learned that truth I was free to stay home, where I found out how much more rewarding it was to have extra time with my wife and kids. Since that period in my life, I've thanked Michael time and time again for helping me learn this truth.

Like all the other negative emotions we've discussed, loneliness can draw us closer to God. How? *First, we need to know why we are lonely.* Most often we are wishing we had someone near us to share our life experiences. We want someone to return to us the same level of affection we wish to give to another. Although the desire for companionship is natural and good, expecting others to meet all our needs can lead to frustration. Even "best friends" and spouses have limits to the amount of time they can spend with us.

Second, while we're feeling lonely, we need to recognize that we are treating God the same way we feel life is treating us. Just as we want someone in God's creation to return our affection, God wants us to return to him the affection he pours out on us. Lonely days and cold winter evenings can depress us. But they also give us time to hear God's gentle whisper—if we listen closely—which calls us to look into the eyes of the One who said, "Never will I leave you; never will I forsake you" (Hebrews 13:5).

Third, we need to return our mind and spirit to the Lord by praying something like this: "Lord, I know that you want all of my heart and soul and mind focused on you as the source of my life. I keep forgetting this and I continually try to recharge my life with your creation. But at this very moment I look to you as my only God. You are my source of lasting life. Lord, you know how I desire to share my life with someone, either a good friend or a mate. I ask you to bring that person into my life, but I'm willing to wait however long is necessary to have your best. And I only want to see this person as overflow, because I want you to continue to be my very best friend. In the meantime show me how to enrich my relationship with you and with those around me."

For some, loneliness may last longer than expected. Our prayer needs to persist as long as loneliness lasts. If loneliness doesn't disappear quickly, we may be tempted to rely on tranquilizers or other artificial means to counteract it—but depending on an aspect of creation will only allow loneliness to entrench itself more deeply. On the other hand, the more we recognize Christ as the source of life and the more we see his faithfulness, the sooner joy and peace will replace loneliness. Plus, *reaching out to others* increases our joy. One of the best ways to find meaningful friendships is to be the kind of friend to others that *we* would like to have.

Anger—Someone or Something Is Blocking My Goal

Occasionally I see this message on my computer screen: "A fatal error has occurred." Like Larry, I freeze, wondering what to do, or if my computer can even recover from this trauma. In marriage, anger is a "fatal error" if not corrected. Therefore, I want to spend a little extra time here, because understanding anger and applying the antidote to anger (which we'll reveal in the next chapter) will go a long way toward building a healthy, happy marriage.

Anger is a secondary emotion that usually comes from one of three sources: **fear, frustration, and hurt feelings**. We all experience these three emotions to some degree daily. By recognizing them early, using the tools we've explored in the last few pages, we can avoid getting angry.

Let me hurry to say that anger isn't always a bad emotion. There are times when anger is appropriate. It can motivate us to do great things—to deal with an injustice or to solve a problem. Sometimes women are afraid when they see their husband have a flash of anger, not realizing that this is an important way for him to have the energy to deal with a crisis. But such anger should never last long, and it *must* be controlled. Unchecked anger begins to settle deep within a person, literally tying him or her up in knots inside. And the longer those knots stay and multiply within a person, the more likely it is that the anger will spill over onto a spouse or others. And that is definitely dangerous.

Anger can erupt at any moment, and it's not always directed at a person. Sometimes we get angry at circumstances, such as a construction detour. The anger we express is evidence that we expect our environment to cooperate with us and to meet our needs. As mentioned earlier, we expect people, things, and work to add something to our lives. We're frustrated because we believe we're about to lose something we thought was secure. Or we realize we may not gain something we had expected to gain.

Before a woman marries, she often has clear expectations concerning her future husband. He will communicate all his goals, expectations, and feelings; he will comfort and hold her when she needs him; he will make her feel special.

After three or four years of marriage, however, some of these women may conclude that it would have been less painful to remain single. Their blocked expectations are often reflected in anger and expressed in explosive outbursts or nagging irritation. Other women may hold their anger inside so that only their pastors or psychiatrists know for sure that it's there. Those counselors are the ones who will see the damage caused by repressed anger.

The same thing is true for men—wives and children may frustrate their personal expectations and drain their emotional energy.

One father we know has been furious with his son for three years because he married a girl from a different social class. What the father won't admit is that his anger is actually a reflection of his own self-centered expectations.

When people and things frustrate our personal goals, anger results. My anger level has dropped significantly over the last several years as I've realized that no person or thing can take away what God has given me. If I lose something of material worth, I know God can replace it if I really need it. So I can relax without feeling compelled to manipulate my circumstances.

I'm not completely free from anger, however. I still tend to use people for my own advantage by setting secret goals for them. When they don't cooperate, I can become frustrated and angry. A few years ago, a publisher asked me to write a book about parenting. Up until then, all of my books had concentrated on marriage. I discussed it with Norma and the children, and they agreed I should do the project. We believed this book could help parents stay in harmony with their children, build their children's self-worth, and help them attain their God-given potential.

In the months that followed, there were some days when my children were disrespectful or unmotivated or testy with each other—in other words, they were normal children. On several occasions, I became angry, thinking that if anyone got wind that things weren't perfect in the Smalley home, my reputation would be ruined. So I lectured my children—until I stopped and thought about what I was doing. Then I realized I was standing in the wrong line again, expecting fulfillment from the people who would be reading this book rather than from God.

We have a saying in our house: "Am I making you angry, or am I revealing your self-centeredness?" With three honest children and a very honest wife, I must often admit that my own self-centeredness is at the core of a problem or disagreement.

People do not really make us angry. We may think they make us angry, but most of the time they simply reveal our own selfishness. What usually makes us angry is our lack of control over people and circumstances.

If I get angry at someone who insults me and deliberately tries to make me angry, I am making a personal decision. This person cannot *make* me angry. Unless I have expectations that he or she will give me something or will not take something important from me, I won't get angry. When I'm angry, I'm using people! So once again, anger reveals self-centeredness. I am angry because someone does not think of me the way I want him or her to think of me.

Under similar circumstances, parents often become angry at their children. If a child does something to embarrass a parent in front of the parent's adult friends, the parent often becomes angry, because adults (just like teens) want their friends to think well of them. The fear of losing social status or approval has spurred many an angry reaction.

One of the most difficult lessons for many of us to learn is to stop trying to gain the approval of others. Expecting to find our true self-image reflected in the opinion of others is like going into a house of mirrors to find out what we really look like. Each person, like each mirror, will tell us something different. One person may admire us for being "open-minded," but someone else may criticize us for "having no convictions." One person may tell us our new outfit is "divine," but someone else might comment, "I had no idea they made outfits like that in your size."

To deal with anger we must come to grips with the fact that we are *not* all-powerful. Until we can see people and circumstances through the eyes of a sovereign God, we will never be free from trying to control what others do to us and think about us.

Yet not all anger is directed toward others. Many times anger is our disgust at our own ineptitude. Once after speaking to a group of more than four hundred men, I berated myself on the drive home. "Smalley, how could you give such a lousy talk? Why in the world did you use that stupid illustration? No one laughed, and it didn't even fit in your outline. They must think you're a real jerk. There goes your reputation!"

In the middle of my mental tirade, I recognized what I was doing and shifted into a prayer: "Lord, thank you that I'm angry and disgusted with myself. Being accepted by those men has nothing to do with my fulfillment. I thank you for loving me and filling me and being so faithful to me for so many years. I want to improve my speaking skills, Lord, and I plan to do that. But I know those skills have nothing to do with you and me."

Then I put some Christian music in my tape deck and sang praise songs the rest of the way home. It took about ten minutes for the anger to subside and for me to feel free, ready to continue with life. I could have spent days feeling like a failure, but instead I used the opportunity to learn more about myself and about God.

RIGHTEOUS ANGER—IS THERE SUCH A THING?

Loving anger is a legitimate form of this usually negative emotion, but I rarely see it in myself or others. Righteous anger is spawned by injustice to another and motivates us to help, not harm, both the victim and the offender. For instance, if someone you know is robbed and beaten, righteous anger would grieve with the victim and gently guide that person back to emotional health. It would also grieve over the sickness of the attacker and, if possible, firmly and directly love that person to wholeness.

Although there are times that call for righteous indignation, those who are honest must admit that most of our anger is the result of self-centeredness. If we are willing, however, we can learn to use this anger to strengthen our relationship with God.

USING ANGER IN A POSITIVE WAY

First, we need to thank God for the message that shows us the connection between our anger and our selfish expectations. Thanksgiving is an expression of trust and obedience. It's a way of saying we want to follow God's way rather than our own.

Second, we need to determine why we're angry. Blocked goals are the most common cause of anger, and anger over blocked goals unmasks our selfish nature.

Third, we need to admit our self-centeredness. The promise of 1 John 1:9–10 is that if we *confess* our sin (of selfishness), God is faithful to forgive us and to purify us. If we think we're not sinners—if we rationalize our anger and insist that we're not being selfish—we lie and the truth is not in us.

We may feel that admitting our selfish ways degrades us, but being aware of natural tendencies has nothing to do with personal worth. Some people think that to confess means they must constantly chant the refrain "for such a worm as I." That is not God's message! However, if we desire a close, dependent relationship with Jesus Christ, we must admit daily, and sometimes hourly, that we are tempted to use an aspect of God's creation to charge our battery. Sometimes we may even surrender to that temptation and become angry when the created thing doesn't fulfill our expectations.

Anger imprisons some people. Those who are physically violent or verbally abusive in their anger, or who are overly critical of themselves and others, very likely will need more help than I can offer in a few pages of a book. Never hesitate to ask for help from qualified Christian counselors and pastors. Your willingness to face the problem and deal with it is a sign of strength. Also, a number of excellent books can help you further understand why people continue in their anger and how you can help break the vicious cycle. I've listed some of them at the end of this book.

Fourth, we need to pray a simple but meaningful prayer expressing to God that we realize he is the source of life. Here are some examples:

- Lord, whether or not I make it to my appointment on time has nothing to do with my fulfillment.
- Lord, the fact that Norma bought white bread rather than whole wheat does not mean I cannot have a fulfilling life.

- Lord, having to take the time to remove Mike's bike from the driveway cannot rob me of your joy.
- Lord, buying the wrong part for this repair job means I'll lose a few minutes, but that won't drain my energy. So what if I have to drive back to the store? It won't mean a thing a year from now.

For many people, it is the little inconveniences like those listed above that bring on an angry response. But anger can also be a response to much more serious issues.

Over the past several years Norma and I have seen many people with deep emotional struggles resulting from tragic circumstances: a woman whose husband had abandoned her and their four school-age children; a man who had given all of his savings (including his retirement fund money) to a "Christian" builder who left town with the money and left behind thousands of dollars of debts; a young woman who waited with a chapel full of guests for a groom who never showed up; and a corporate manager who worked for years to reach the top, only to have his company bought out in a hostile takeover, leaving him jobless at the age of sixty-one.

People, money, things, career. The loss of these caused severe hurt that led to bitter anger for each of these people. But when they discovered the true source of lasting life and recognized their anger as a message warning them that they were operating without the power of a sovereign God who could *more than* compensate for their loss, they were able to deal with their loss instead of letting it devastate them.

We helped each one through weeks of dealing with the necessary grief. Then, when they were ready, we walked with them into a personal, healing relationship with Jesus Christ.

Martin Luther once said about temptation, "You cannot keep birds from flying over your head, but you can keep them from building a nest in your hair." The same is true with anger.

We cannot control the circumstances that make us angry, but we *can* control how we respond to them. We can resist the temptation to let our circumstances make us angry.

Envy, jealousy, lust, hurt feelings, worry, loneliness, and anger. This is by no means an exhaustive list of negative emotions. We could examine many others, but the principles for achieving victory are all very similar—because the underlying cause is basically the same. If we really want to eliminate most negative emotions, then we must *go to the source.* I'm warning you, you may not find this pretty. But if you'll confront this common human issue, you will free yourself to truly enjoy God as the source of joy.

CHAPTER EIGHT

Solving the Problem at the Source

IN THE MIDST OF an author tour for my book *Making Love Last Forever*, we stopped at a retirement home. While there *were* a few couples living there, there were even more widows and widowers, so I wondered why we were there promoting a book on marriage. However, I had a delightful time visiting with a ninety-year-old woman. After we'd talked for a few minutes, thinking maybe she'd buy a book for her grandchildren, I asked her, "Do you know who I am?"

With a sweet smile, she answered, "No, but if you go to the front desk, they'll tell you who you are!"

Certainly I was in no danger of getting a big head that day.

Around that same time, back home in Branson, I had some landscaping done on my property. I was fascinated by the huge bulldozer being used for some of the work. I guess I'm still a kid at heart; I longed for a chance to drive the bulldozer. Since the contractor had to leave the machine on my property over the weekend, I asked him if he would mind if I took it for a spin. With permission granted, I took off on a wonderful ride. I managed to knock down some trees in the woods on my property. In the process, I accidentally knocked over a section of my fence, but that didn't bother me, for I believed the land on the other side was part of my property. So I went ahead and cleared out a few more trees.

The next day, my neighbor down the street came by. After introducing ourselves and shaking hands, he asked me, "Did you happen to see anyone driving a bulldozer on my property?"

Well, I was sure I hadn't gone off my property, so I answered, "No. What happened?"

"Well, someone knocked down my fence and a number of my trees." He pointed in the direction where I'd been driving.

With a gulp I realized that perhaps I wasn't quite so sure of my property lines after all. Immediately, I thought I would blame my contractor, saying something like, "You know, you just can't get good help these days." In the next instant, I knew I had to tell the truth. With embarrassment I admitted what I'd done and made arrangements to fix his fence. I also agreed to cut up the trees for his winter firewood supply.

I tell both of these stories in my seminars, and they never fail to get laughs. But they serve a greater purpose than loosening up a crowd. They remind me of why people listen to me—and it's *not* because I'm any great expert. I don't have a Ph.D. in marriage counseling. Unlike researchers such as Dr. John Gottman and Dr. Scott Stanley, I haven't done a linear study on hundreds of couples over twenty years to observe what makes for healthy and unhealthy marital interaction. I can't point to articles I've written in prestigious academic journals. The primary credentials I offer to audiences are my mistakes—and the lessons I've learned from them.

Such stories also remind me of another important truth, for they reveal the source of my joy. Suppose my encounter with the ninety-year-old woman hurt my feelings. Because I was supposedly on a tour to promote my book, I could have demanded of my manager that he not waste my time with such appearances.

That sort of reaction would be an error message, warning me that I was looking to people to charge my battery.

Or consider the bulldozer story—I could have become envious of my neighbor's property. Then I'd have known that I was looking to things (land and trees) to make me happy.

At their core, all of the negative emotions we've examined do one thing for me: They unmask my self-centeredness, which is pride.

Pride Is Expecting God's Creation to Meet My Needs

Pride thinks the world revolves around me. And it's deadly in marriage. Pride results in husband and wife waiting for each other, or things, or career to charge their emotional batteries. The presence of negative emotions gives evidence that those expectations are unfulfilled.

When a couple feels envy toward a neighbor or friends who have bought their dream home, husband and wife should realize they are really thinking they can't be happy without a bigger salary or better job that would allow them to buy a bigger home. They rarely consider that their marriage might experience greater pressure if their dream were to be fulfilled.

When a wife is jealous because the husband of her best friend always remembers *his* wife's anniversary and birthday and does special things to honor her, she is receiving a warning message—"Error: You expect your husband to make you happy by doing those same things."

When a man feels lust for a woman who's not his wife, he's really saying, "My mate doesn't meet my needs. She doesn't listen to me and understand me like the pretty secretary at work does. She's not as witty or intelligent as the woman in the marketing department. To be complete, I need someone more than God and the mate he has given to me."

Do you see the pattern? It's the same with envy, jealousy, lust, hurt feelings, fear or worry, loneliness, and anger. Each of these emotions, at its core, reveals our selfishness. They tell us that we are expecting someone or something else to meet our goals, but they aren't cooperating.

All seven of these emotions have their root in pride. And as long as I concentrate on *me* and *my* emotions, I sever my connection with God and his resources. Sure, husband and wife can work through these things on their own, and non-Christians do it all the time. But it's much easier and healthier when both recognize their pride and yield their expectations to God.

Honesty Is the Best Policy

It's tough, but this is where we must be brutally honest. It's not pretty. But if we play games here, we will miss out on life as God intended. A couple of years ago my coauthor, Al, came home one evening after he and his wife, Jo, had been at a party with some friends. It just so happened that there were a couple of attractive, intelligent single women at the party, and Al had proceeded to have a rather animated discussion with them. As Jo and Al were going to bed that night, Jo commented, "You sure were full of yourself tonight!" To which Al lovingly responded, "What else did you expect me to be full of?"

Needless to say, Al didn't get a very affirming response to his smart-aleck comment. But Jo's honest assessment started Al on a spiritual journey in which he had to recognize his pride and take it to God. Over the next few days, during his personal devotions, he read a little book by Andrew Murray called *Humility: The Beauty of Holiness*. Al wrote this quote from the book in his journal: "Humility is not something which we bring to God, or he bestows; it is simply the sense of entire nothingness, which comes when we see how truly God is all, and in which we make way for God to be all."[1]

---

[1]Andrew Murray, *Humility: The Beauty of Holiness* (Springdale, Pa.: Whitaker House, 1982), 12.

Here is the same lesson I had to learn: *God is the source of life.* Pride, in essence, tells God that we know better than he does what makes a quality life. The marriage experts are saying the same thing: Believing that any of your own opinions, thinking patterns, or concerns are somewhat better, higher, or more important than your mate's is the biggest killer of love! Thus Al came to the point where he had to admit the problem his wife identified: that, at least in part, his self-worth came from being able to hold the attention of an attractive female. There was nothing wrong in carrying on a conversation with someone, but he'd crossed the line—the love of God plus the admiration and love of his wife weren't enough; he felt he needed more.

It's hard to admit such shortcomings. Yet our lives and marriages will be enriched when we allow God to shine his light into these secret corners of our lives. Al didn't realize how important this lesson would be in his work. Shortly after the incident at the party, a decision was made to discontinue the publishing operation Al had been heading up for a major ministry. This was a work he had spent years building, and over the next year it would be systematically disassembled and replaced with a very different model.

Fortunately, Al shared this news with his wife, so Jo was able to pray with him and support him during their nightly walks when they debriefed about the day's events. Often husbands withhold their thoughts and fears and frustrations about work from the person closest to them. Some men think that two "grunts" covers their entire day. The wife will ask, "Honey, did your day go okay?" All she'll get in response is a weary "Uh huh."

When problems at the office leave a husband brooding at home, the wife wonders what is wrong. Often the problem is that the man is drawing his meaning and life from his job, and the job is being most uncooperative. If he won't talk about it, however, the wife may have a different interpretation. She may think he's upset with her, or wonder why he can't keep work and family separate and simply enjoy her and their home life.

Al thought he'd gotten beyond such struggles. Intellectually, he knew his life didn't depend on what he did. He plunged enthusiastically into the major restructuring of his department. So, he was surprised at some of the emotions that assaulted him in the middle of the night, and for several weeks he suffered from bouts of insomnia. One night, in an unusually vivid dream, he realized he had suffered a loss and had not admitted it and allowed himself time to grieve.

Part of the healing process was recognizing that an important part of his life had changed. As he processed that reality, he was able to pray: "Lord, thank you that my life is not about my career. Rather, it's about knowing and pleasing you. When I take my eyes off of me and let you energize me, you give me work that provides meaning. But I know *you* are the source of my life, not my work."

The battles Al fought during this period could have hurt his marriage. Jo could have been jealous of her husband's posturing; instead, she let God deal with him. Al had to be honest that this was a constant struggle, and remember that *God* was the source of life, not a human being's approval. The change in work responsibilities could have torn husband and wife apart if Al had insisted his work was what gave his life meaning. But his depression was a warning light reminding Al that God was the source of life, not his career.

Al and Jo had another recent reminder that their marriage is not about people or things. For seven years, they lived in a beautiful house with a view of the mountains in Colorado Springs. Then they did the un-American thing and sold it—and bought a smaller, more modest, and less expensive home. Jo admits she briefly struggled with how people would perceive this switch. Many of their friends have far larger, more prestigious homes. But she and Al believe their life comes from God, not from a house. In order to have maximum flexibility so they can serve God and people, they want to be debt-free as soon as possible. So while this downward move may not make sense to some of their friends, it was the right move for them.

Dealing with the issue of pride may make us squirm. No one wants to admit being proud. Yet it *must* be addressed, and sometimes there's no delicate way to do it. A few years ago, Mary came to my office and asked for help in her struggles with her husband. As I listened to her complain about his harsh, demanding, and insensitive ways, I noticed her face reflected a hard, deep-seated resentment. She spent a great deal of time describing his lack of love. He demanded that she dress in a certain way so he would always look good with her. Once when she scratched the car fender he treated her like a child by taking her "toy" away until she "learned how to drive."

She left herself wide-open when she paused to say, "I'm really hurting over my husband's treatment. Is there anything I can do to relieve the pain?" Now you need to realize this was early in my ministry. Today I would probably not use such a confrontational approach unless I knew the person better. I forced Mary to face something she didn't want to face when I asked her, "How self-centered do you think you are?"

First amazement, then irritation at my brash question spread across her face. "I'm not very self-centered at all," she responded. "Most of my time is spent taking care of the children or my husband. I have almost no time for myself."

Not sure where this would lead, I asked Mary to do some homework. Her assignment was to write down every time she was angry or had hurt feelings, frustrations, or fears—especially with her husband—and to ask herself *what she was personally losing* that might cause such hurt or anger. Mary agreed to return in a week and reveal the results.

During our next appointment Mary confessed that for the first time she realized how many things she unconsciously expected of her husband, her children, and her environment. She had filled three pages with incidents and discovered that *every time* she was angry or hurt, someone had denied her something she wanted.

When I asked her again how self-centered she thought she was, she lowered her head and answered, "*Very* self-centered."

I immediately confessed, "I, too, am self-centered. Frankly, it's a toss-up as to who is more selfish. But I suspect I probably have you beat!"

Admitting we are selfish is not easy. I like to be thought of as a caring, compassionate, giving person who always looks out for the best interests of others. But in reality, my best attempts to be righteous are like filthy rags, according to the prophet Isaiah (see Isaiah 64:6).

We all need to admit our self-centeredness because out of such an admission comes the freedom to refocus our expectations away from God's creation and to God himself.

The Solution to Pride

So what can we do about this problem? I would suggest that in a marriage relationship, each person must first address this problem individually. You may get a reaction even stronger than Al had to his wife if you volunteer to reveal the pride in your partner. However, if you're willing, you may choose to solicit the help of your spouse. Let's look at how to root out this problem.

ASK GOD TO REVEAL YOUR PRIDE AND THEN ADMIT IT

The first step is to recognize the problem. God has many ingenious ways of revealing pride. One is our *negative emotions,* if we're willing to use them as warning messages. I've trained myself over the years, whenever I feel hurt or angry or jealous, to ask, "What am I expecting from someone or something, or what am I afraid of losing?"

Another means is found in Paul's letter to the Philippians: "Do nothing out of selfish ambition or vain conceit, but in humility consider others better than yourselves" (Philippians 2:3). The attitude we are to have is that of Jesus Christ, who modeled humility by setting aside his rights as God and becoming a man. It's usually easy to recognize my pride when I compare my attitudes to those of Christ.

But honestly, I often don't want to admit there is a problem. So I need the help of others to reveal my blind spots of pride. I've invited my family to ask me what my emotions of anger are revealing about me. They can say, "Dad, is your anger telling you that you are expecting me, not God, to meet your need?" In other words, when I'm angry or hurt, their question reminds me that those emotions usually reveal that my focus is on what I'm not getting or what I think I'm losing.

Sometimes, my family members can be rather blunt. Recently my youngest son, who is working toward his Ph.D. in counseling, showed me some new research about Attention Deficit Disorder, or A.D.D. As I looked over the material, I realized it described a lot of the problems I had as a young child and teenager. I struggled in school; I was easily distracted and never really found my way in a classroom setting. Now I understood why.

Right about this time my daughter Kari was trying to tell me something very important. However, I was distracted—I don't even remember what drew my attention away from her. Kari grabbed me and forced me to look at her: "Dad, this is very important. Pay attention."

Well, I laughed and dismissed her urgency by saying, "I'm sorry, but you know I can't help it. That's just my A.D.D. coming out."

Kari, with great perception, said, "No, Dad. That's *not* A.D.D. You have R.U.D.E."

Ouch! She was right. I immediately gave her my full attention.

When confronted with the truth, I could have been defensive and tried to deny what she was saying. But as James says in the first chapter of his letter, that's like looking at your face in a mirror, then immediately forgetting what you saw. The apostle Paul says love "is not rude" (1 Corinthians 13:5). I was being rude; thus I was not being loving to my daughter.

ASK FOR FORGIVENESS

To ask for forgiveness is hard, because pride, by its very nature, doesn't want to let go. It wants to prove it's in the right. Men in particular seem to struggle with this issue. Often, even when they recognize the importance of asking for forgiveness, they will *react* at first, then later admit they were wrong. Even if it's delayed, admitting your pride is better than trying to cover it up. After all, our wives do know better!

Norma has told me she prefers I stay away from the laundry, for I have a habit of messing things up. However, if I'm going to help, she has instructed me to put her clothes in the dryer for no more than five minutes, then hang them up.

One day I observed that Norma was washing a load of her clothes, and since she was busy on the phone, I thought I would surprise her by keeping the clothes moving through the process. So when the washing cycle was finished, I removed the load from the washer and put it in the dryer for five minutes. I really did intend to take them out and hang them up to finish drying. But something "distracted" me and two hours later, I remembered, "Oh no, Norma's clothes!" I rushed back to the dryer, but it was too late to prevent the damage. For a moment, I was tempted to put them back in the washer, thinking she'd never know. I guess I wanted to believe I could rehydrate them.

With fear and trepidation, I told my wife, "I have good news and bad news. The bad news: I dried your clothes that were in the washer!"

"What!" I immediately sensed the tension rising.

"But there's good news," I quickly interjected. "Taylor [our five-year-old granddaughter] has a whole new wardrobe!"

Humor didn't solve the problem, but it did defuse it a little. I asked for her forgiveness and handed her my wallet as a gesture of repentance. She responded that it takes a long time to find these kinds of clothes. Still, she knew I was willing to do whatever was necessary to make things right.

SEEK TO FORGIVE OTHERS WHO HAVE HURT YOU

You know what's amazing? When we admit that God is our source for life, it's hard to get hurt by others.

Of all the emotions we've explored, I believe anger causes the most problems. Unresolved anger is a cancer in the marriage relationship. Anger may not even be caused by the spouse, but the spouse will surely feel the results. Anger develops when negative emotions are allowed to fester. The rage a wife may express to her husband could have its roots in being abused as a girl. The hostility a wife may sense in her husband may trace back to the divorce of his parents when he was a little boy.

There's only one way to cure this cancer—forgiveness. Without forgiveness, the injured person will spew anger on those around him or her. And those people we love—our kids, for example–become more likely to grow up and spray anger on others. At some point we must break the chain—and forgiveness is the only way I know to do it.

I should emphasize that by forgiveness I do *not* mean forgetting what was done to you. It may or may not mean you are reconciled to the person who hurt you. What forgiveness provides is freedom—release from the pain that binds you.

So how can we carry out this forgiveness? First, allow yourself to *grieve your loss.* You need to realize that something *was* taken from you. The person who hurt you was wrong. The man who abused you sinned against you. When your parents divorced, you suffered. Don't deny the pain.

A spouse can help greatly by providing a listening ear. When Al's dream job was eliminated, he immediately plunged ahead with the work he had to do. But his insomnia and vivid dreams revealed his need to grieve. Jo was very helpful, allowing him on their nightly walks to talk about what he had lost and how he felt about it. A husband can do the same with his wife, letting her talk about the hurt she felt when someone offended or disrespected her.

Second, *seek to understand* why your offender hurt you. This is a most important step in untying the knots of anger. One of the more dramatic examples I've seen happened when I spoke on a university campus. My first lecture was to a group of faculty members, and I was very nervous. In the middle of my talk, a woman got up and announced, "I don't have to listen to any more of this nonsense," and she stormed out of the room. Needless to say, I was embarrassed. Then I was angry, thinking, *How could she humiliate me like this!*

Often in our marriage relationship we may assume we did something wrong when a spouse vents, but there may a completely unrelated reason for the anger that has nothing to do with us at all. After I calmed down, I was curious why this woman would act the way she did toward me. So I found out where she worked, went to her office, and asked for five minutes of her time. She was reluctant to give me even five minutes, and she thought I was crazy when I said, "I want to thank you for what you did. I speak a lot, and I'm always curious if people are helped by what I say. So when you got up and left, I was curious. What did you see or hear that made you so mad?"

Within two minutes, I learned that in reality this woman was angry with her administrator. Something I said—she couldn't remember what it was specifically—fanned her emotion. For several minutes, she spewed out complaints against her boss while I simply listened. It didn't take long to realize that I wasn't the cause of her anger. But she couldn't express those angry, hurt feelings to her boss. So I, a person who'd disappear from campus in a couple of days, very likely never to be seen by this woman again, was the lucky recipient of her venting.

As I rose to leave, this woman asked, "How many more times are you speaking here?"

I told her I was speaking two more times.

"I want to introduce you to those groups." In less than fifteen minutes, this woman had become my friend. And it happened because I took the time to understand what was really bothering her.

Third, *release* the person who offended you so you have no reason to seek revenge. I suggest you do this out loud, even if you can't do it in person. My brother died of a heart attack when he was only fifty years old, and for many weeks I was angry at him because he had refused to get medical help until it was too late. After trying to understand why he had been so stubborn, I realized I had to let it go. Alone in a room, I said, "Ronnie, I forgive you for not getting medical attention and for causing me this pain." Just by performing that little ceremony, there was a tremendous sense of release—the anger was gone.

The purpose of granting forgiveness is to say, in essence, "I don't expect anything more from you." And if I don't expect anything more from the person who hurt me, then I can return to the source of my joy, who is God, who loves me perfectly.

THANK GOD THAT HE IS THE SOURCE OF LIFE

Thanksgiving acknowledges that God is the source of life. Frankly, it's so much more enjoyable to live with a thankful person. And there's so much to thank God for—if we know where to look.

While I was writing the original version of *Joy That Lasts*, I received a phone call from the producer of the Focus on the Family radio program, featuring Dr. James Dobson. My book, *The Key to Your Child's Heart*, had recently been published, and the producer wanted to interview me to see if I might be a good candidate to appear on the program. Naturally, I was excited. Every author of a Christian book wants to be interviewed by Dr. Dobson.

A few weeks later, I flew to California and taped two shows. A few weeks after that, I received a tape of the program just before it was scheduled to air. I eagerly popped the cassette into my car tape player. Within a few minutes, I was horrified. In my enthusiasm for the subject, I had eagerly responded to Dr. Dobson's comments with words like, "Yes," "That's right!" "Uh-huh." Without realizing it, I was speaking over him, interrupting what he had to say.

Within days, letters started arriving from listeners. One woman angrily informed me that she would never listen to me again because I was so rude. I was terribly embarrassed. "Lord, I wish I'd known what I was doing," I prayed. "I'm embarrassed. But I know that being on Focus on the Family is not the source of my life. Regardless of what others think, I know you charge my battery. Thank you for this reminder that my life comes from you, not what others think. And Lord, help me to remember to hold my tongue when others are talking."

That embarrassment returns every three years or so, when Focus on the Family re-airs the broadcast. Each time it's a reminder to again thank God that he is the source of my life.

In summary, every negative emotion allows us to discover selfishness, which allows us to recognize again that only God provides lasting energy for our battery—a truth for which we can always be thankful.

Pride Is Something You Can Afford to Lose

In this area of pride, I have plenty of personal examples. One of the most embarrassing came when I thought I was reaching a new pinnacle in my career. Steve Scott had produced a very successful infomercial on marriage that enjoyed a three-year run. Then the response rates started dropping, and Steve suggested we create a new product on parenting. He recommended we record a two-minute commercial and test it.

This suggestion was an answer to prayer. I'd been standing in line for months, asking God to give me a platform to teach on the subject of parenting. So naturally, I thanked God for opening this door.

I flew to Hollywood and spent an entire day recording the commercial with celebrity Burl Ives. It took hours to film because I was so nervous. Everything had to be done perfectly; I had to walk to a certain spot, sit a certain way in a chair, smile, read a teleprompter, and do my lines perfectly. I lost count of the number of takes; it felt like a hundred.

After we were done, I wrote to all of my friends and family members, plus my national board, telling them to be sure to watch for this commercial. I just knew it would be a success; after all, the marriage infomercial had done so well. It didn't take long for Steve to call with the results of the test. "Gary, I'm sorry, but it was a total bomb. Only thirty people called for the product."

That's thirty people in the entire nation! And my friends were calling to find out how this venture was going. I had to tell them they wouldn't see it again. The whole situation was embarrassing—the recording session itself, the fact that so many people knew, and most of all, the fact that I *thought* God was answering my prayer. Why, I wondered, had he raised my hopes like this? Or had I misunderstood? Maybe this wasn't God's work at all.

It took a couple of days to work through the embarrassment. Several times I went off by myself and prayed. "God, how did I miss this by so far? It looked to me like it was going to be such a great way to expand our ministry to parents all over the country. How could this happen? What did I do wrong?"

After a while, my prayer changed, and I began to thank God. "Lord, I need to go on with my life. So I'm thanking you for this experience. Thank you that I was humiliated and embarrassed, for I know this trial is deepening my relationship with you, and it will make me more like Christ and more loving toward others." Then I got back in line and began praying again about an opportunity to teach parenting principles to others.

What are you afraid of losing in life? Is there anything or anyone you think you can't live without? At some point, you may need to face the reality. When you do, there will be a sense of loss, to be sure. But God can fill that void with himself. Daily we can go to the source of life—we can return to the source of joy.

Knowing how to use natural negative emotions to strengthen our relationship with God has tremendous value, but think how great it would be if we could also use everyday trials, both small and great, to draw us closer to God. The next two chapters uncover one of the most exciting truths I have learned: how trials, hardships, and difficulties can be the doorway to a richer life, how they can lead us to live in the center of God's will. Believe it or not, trials can make us more loving. And perhaps best of all, trials can even increase our sense of personal worth.

Talk about a *supercharged* life—this is it!

CHAPTER NINE

The Secret of Turning Trials into Benefits

I HAD JUST FINISHED speaking to a roomful of professional football players and their wives when a striking blond woman approached me. Her husband stood back as the woman, her eyes red, spoke to me. I had to strain to hear her words. "I can't go on . . . ," she said, and started crying. "I feel terrible about myself. I can't respond to my husband. I can't love my daughter. I'm no good to anyone."

As I glanced at her husband, a veteran National Football League player, he indicated with his eyes and expression that he was at a loss to know what to do. *Could I please help his wife?* he seemed to plead. I suggested that we leave the room and find a place to talk.

In private I was let in on a few details. Jill was born into a wealthy home, but when she was three years old her father deserted the family, leaving her mother and brothers destitute. As a young girl she was raped by her uncle, then her brothers. As a teenager and young woman, she struggled through a number of relationships with males who took advantage of her sexually.

Jill finally married, but the scars of her traumatic past remained. She found herself increasingly withdrawing from her husband, unable to accept any kind of affection. Moreover, she seemed drawn to the kind of friends who only wanted to take advantage of her. It was as though she was unable to run from danger.

As her husband caressed her hand, Jill said: "When I was a little girl, everyone said I was very beautiful. I'll never forget at a family picnic being told, 'You're so beautiful, it must be your purpose in life to satisfy the sexual urges of men.'"

The need of this couple was so great that we agreed to meet in Phoenix, where I was living at the time. They flew out and spent several hours talking. Gradually, the tide began to turn. What we discovered literally changed this woman's life and saved their marriage.

Marriage often comes with a great deal of baggage on the part of one or both partners. It doesn't matter how successful they appear on the outside. This woman was a former model; her husband was a successful pro athlete. They had everything the world considers of value—a gorgeous mate, lots of money and the things it can buy, and great careers. Plus, they were Christians. Looking at them from the outside, no one would suspect there was this kind of intense pain in their lives.

How do we work through such pain? It's fine to say that God is the source of life—indeed he is. But we also need to understand why we suffer. We need answers for the pain we have in our past as well as in the present. That's why I'm so excited about the truth we're about to explore, for God has provided a way to turn all negative things in life into something very positive. Further, when anyone applies this truth, their self-worth rises, for they discover how much God loves them, and how they can give genuine love to others.

Many of us have been tricked into believing the world's viewpoint that suffering is bad and should be avoided whenever possible. The words of the apostle Paul say otherwise: "In all things God works for the good . . ." (Romans 8:28). How can any good be found in a life-threatening illness, desertion by a father, bankruptcy, natural disaster, child abuse, or any tragic circumstance? Intellectually we believe the biblical promise that in *all things* God works for good, but most of us have wondered at one time or another what *good* could possibly exist in our own personal trials.

I am convinced that the promise of Romans 8:28 is true in *every* case. In all my years of counseling and study, I have never found an exception, but it took me a long time to discover how to *find* the good in each trial. The concepts in this chapter have transformed my life and the lives of many others.

Turning Lead into Gold

To understand this incredible truth, think of a fulfilling, satisfying, enjoyable life—a life filled with peace and love and energy because it is focused on Jesus Christ. This life places the highest value on God and shows it by honoring him in worship. This life also realizes that the second most important thing is honoring others, and so it is dedicated to loving and serving people. The person possessing this life also realizes she can only love others to the degree she recognizes that she is herself a special gift of God. And because God doesn't make junk, this person knows she has great value. These three things are the treasure of life—loving and honoring *God*, loving and honoring *others* because our needs are met by God, and recognizing the *value* of our own lives, which are created by God.

These three things of great value can all be damaged by sin. For example, we damage our relationship with God by our actions or words, by ignoring him, by doing natural human things that exclude him. However, God invites us to restore that relationship by confessing our sins, and he *is* faithful to forgive us, though we may suffer the consequences of our sins.

Likewise, we can enrich the lives of other people by guiding them to a relationship with God. But sometimes those relationships are damaged. We say and do things that are demeaning. We offend people, sometimes without even knowing it. But if our desire is to love God and love others, then we should attempt to repair those relationships as soon as possible.

Sometimes we damage our own sense of value, or it is marred by others. We make mistakes and then condemn ourselves for our stupidity. Or we are demeaned by those who should value us. In the process we forget how valuable we are to God, because *he created us.* How do we repair that damage to our self-worth? That's the critical question of this chapter. It's critical in marriage because, as one leading marriage expert has said, a marriage is only as strong as the weakest partner. If one person suffers from low self-worth, he or she limits how much either partner gains in the relationship.

But there is hope for any individual who is willing to invest a little work searching for God's good. When both husband and wife find this truth, it can revolutionize a marriage. To set up what we're about to learn, imagine being able to see your heart immediately after you become a Christian. The Bible tells us that anyone who is in Christ is a new creation (see 2 Corinthians 5:17). So picture your new heart as a huge nugget of soft, pliable eighteen-karat gold.

After becoming a Christian, sooner or later (usually sooner) we go through trials and difficulties. People offend us, hurt our feelings, or cause us to be fearful. Circumstances of life beat us up, bruising our heart. Add to that all the painful memories from the past—perhaps incest, divorce, loss of a loved one—and those memories add more bruises to our valuable but tender heart. In time, that heart of gold given to us when we met Jesus turns purple. And if it's left unattended, the bruises become hardened and parts of that heart turn into another metal—one called *lead*. What should be gold has become a worthless metal, which is exactly how we feel.

God has designed a process for transforming the lead back into gold—only it's a gold that's even more refined and pure. God can transform our hearts, damaged by the bruises of life, into twenty-four-karat gold!

How is this possible? Let me encourage you to walk through the process with me. You can start by thinking of some things you wish had never happened to you. Can you prioritize them? Pick out one to three things you think are the worst. At this point, you probably can't imagine much, if any, good in these painful memories. How can God turn these bruises, this lead, into twenty-four-karat gold? *Not* by trying to think positively. And *not* by minimizing the pain you feel—it's real! Yet what others meant for evil, God can use for good. Let's look at one example, then examine several portions of Scripture, and then reflect on a few more examples, including that of Jill.

The End of a Career Isn't the End of the World

Monte Johnson, an eight-year veteran with the Oakland Raiders' professional football team, faced the biggest crisis of his life. Would he be cut from the team? Would he be traded? He had five months to worry about it.

Monte never started a game as an undergraduate at the University of Nebraska, but he attracted the attention of pro scouts in an all-star game—and the Raiders drafted him. He went on to become a starting linebacker and played for the Super Bowl champions in 1977. Then tragedy struck. In a preseason game against the Washington Redskins, a teammate accidentally collided with Monte on a kickoff return, destroying the ligaments and cartilage in his knee. While his teammates went on to win the Super Bowl again that year, Monte worked diligently to rehabilitate his knee. But when I saw him the next year, he told me there was a real possibility he would never play football again. Training camp was five months away, but already his anxiety over the situation was straining all of his relationships.

"I have no idea what to do after football," he told me. "I had planned to play at least two more years. Even my wife doesn't understand that my career may be over."

I challenged Monte to do something that at first blush seemed crazy. I asked him to turn his injured knee and possible release from the Raiders into a benefit. To help him start the process, we talked about his options. One was to play football again for the Raiders. Another was to be traded to another team. The third was to retire and go into another line of work. I asked Monte to write down the benefits of all three possibilities. The first one was easy—playing for the Raiders—but it took a while for Monte to see any benefits in the other two options.

I saw Monte again a year later and he couldn't wait to share with me his experience. He had taken time to write down all the benefits he could think of for the two "negative" options—being traded or retiring from pro football. In both possibilities he saw ways to grow spiritually and to minister to other hurting people. Regarding the second of those options, he began getting ideas for developing a business. Plus, if he retired, he would have more time for his family. When he arrived at training camp, he was excited because he knew that *whatever* happened would be for his good. He saw an almost equal number of benefits in all three options.

At summer camp, after a thorough physical exam, the coach told Monte the bad news: His knee was not strong enough to handle the rigors of football and he would have to retire. The first words out of Monte's mouth shocked the coach. "I want to thank God for choosing you to be the instrument to help me discover what God wants me to do," Monte said. "Thank you for eight great years with the Raider organization."

Flabbergasted at such an unusual reaction from a player who had just been cut, the coach could think of nothing more to say.

Monte gave him a hug and thanked him again for his years with the team.

Professional athletes dread retirement. Being told that their career is over at an age when most men are entering the prime of life devastates many of them. What made the difference for Monte was the time he'd spent treasure hunting. He uncovered the benefits and learned to see the experience as an *opportunity* rather than as a trial.

Several months after his release from the Raiders, Monte became involved in a financial counseling and management program to help athletes and other professionals plan for the future—a ministry that has now helped hundreds of people.

Anyone can do what Monte did.

Every problem—great or small—has in it a treasure waiting to be discovered. The secret to successful treasure hunting is understanding two life-changing words: faith and love.

Getting Through Trials Requires Faith

Jesus' teaching about faith will show us its true meaning if we pay attention to how he helped distraught people through their trials. In one situation Jesus praised a Roman soldier for having "great faith"; a few hours later, Jesus rebuked the disciples for exercising "little faith." Let's see if we can determine the difference.

GREAT FAITH VERSUS LITTLE FAITH

Matthew tells of a Roman officer who came to Jesus and said, "Lord, ... my servant lies at home paralyzed and in terrible suffering" (Matthew 8:6). Even though the man made only a statement, not a request, Jesus answered, "'I will go and heal him.' The centurion replied, 'Lord, I do not deserve to have you come under my roof. But just say the word, and my servant will be healed'" (Matthew 8:7–8). Amazed by the centurion's faith, Jesus said to the people around him, "I have not found anyone in Israel with such *great faith*" (Matthew 8:10, italics added).

What prompted this response? In such a religious country how could there be so little faith? What about the Pharisees and the religious leaders? No doubt they were irritated by Jesus' words and proud of the actions that demonstrated their faith. And what about the disciples? Surely *they* had faith.

What the soldier said that so impressed Jesus was, "Lord, I do not deserve to have you come under my roof. But *just say the word,* and my servant will be healed. For I myself am a man *under authority,* with soldiers under me. I tell this one, 'Go!' and he goes; and that one, 'Come,' and he comes. I say to my servant, 'Do this,' and he does it" (Matthew 8:8–9, italics added).

The reason Jesus called the centurion's faith *great* was because the man believed without question that Jesus could heal his servant. He could picture in his mind how Jesus could order the deed done in the same way he ordered his soldiers or servants. Jesus was under the Father's authority just as the centurion was under the authority of the Roman government. People obeyed the centurion because the empire delegated power to him just as the God of the universe delegated power to Jesus. Jesus fulfilled the man's expectation "just as you believed it would" (Matthew 8:13), and his servant was healed that very hour.

It's important to note that Jesus only did the will of his Father (for example, see John 5:19–20), and the Father revealed all things to the Son. Therefore, Jesus saw God healing the servant. The key to faith is *knowing what God is going to do ahead of time.* Of course, God often doesn't reveal what he is going to do to us. So how do we exercise faith? There may be more clues than you suspect.

The story of the centurion stands in stark contrast to an event, probably later that same day, that illustrated the weak faith of the disciples. Jesus told them to get into their boat and to cross over to the other side of the lake. Undoubtedly exhausted from an intense day of ministry, Jesus then fell sound asleep inside the boat.

Halfway across the unpredictable sea, the boat nearly capsized when a fierce storm suddenly arose. Waves crashed over the sides of the boat, and the disciples panicked. In the fury of the wind and rain and waves, they could picture only one scene—a quick trip to the bottom of the lake! In desperation they roused Jesus, who in a word reduced the storm to a gently shimmering sea. Then he rebuked the disciples with these words: "You of *little faith*, why are you so afraid?" (Matthew 8:26, italics added).

Why did the disciples have little faith? How did their faith differ from that of the centurion? The difference was that in the midst of the storm, the disciples forgot that Jesus had said they were going over to the other side of the lake. They pictured themselves drowning, not reaching the dry land of the far shore. They mistakenly assumed that if they were going to arrive safely on the other side they would surely enjoy smooth sailing along the way. They didn't anticipate such fierce trouble en route to their destination. But Jesus had already *seen* the trip and saw them landing safely, because the Father had already revealed it to him.

Treasure in Every Trial

Many of us make the same mistake. During difficult times we forget that God has promised to produce maturity, righteousness, and love through our trials. He has told us to "consider it pure joy … whenever you face trials of many kinds" (James 1:2) and has reminded us that "we live by faith, not by sight" (2 Corinthians 5:7). When waves threaten to capsize our boat, natural thinking takes over and we lose all hope of survival. People with inadequate faith say, "Those promises don't apply to me. God doesn't understand my situation. How can any good come out of all this suffering?" Years after a tragedy, they are lying helplessly at the bottom of the lake covered with barnacles of bitterness instead of walking on the sunny, sandy shore enjoying the fullness of God's blessing.

Many people I counsel suffer from a negative self-image because of the hardships they have endured. Discovering the treasure buried in our trials is the fastest way I know to raise self-worth. God wants us to think well of ourselves because he wants us to love others as we love ourselves. When we devalue ourselves, we hinder our love for others.

Treasure hunting can raise self-worth, no matter what the circumstances.

DISCOVERING TREASURE IN TRIALS

The following exercise is the one I use to discover the treasure in my personal trials. Perhaps it will work for you as well.

Divide a piece of paper into five columns and label the columns as follows: 1. What I Like About Myself; 2. My Past Trials; 3. Support People; 4. Benefits from Trials; 5. Love in Action.

In the first column list at least three things you like about yourself. Some people want to skip this part, perhaps concluding there isn't anything to like about themselves. But don't short-circuit the process. There is something to like in everyone, and we need to see it in order to begin the process of finding the treasure God has for us.

In the second column list the things you don't like about yourself, the things that cause low self-worth. These are the painful experiences that cause anger, bitterness, and varying levels of grief. Some people have told me it's too painful to write down all their trials at one time, so you may prefer to focus on one or two for the moment and deal with others at another time.

In the third column list the people who have helped you through your more serious trials. Something in your past may have been so painful that you needed a professional counselor. Or perhaps you found a friend who prayed with you until you regained your strength after a particularly difficult experience.

In the fourth column list whatever benefits you can think of that came as a result of your trial(s). If you can't think of any at first, remember that for Christians all trials produce various aspects of love, so think of ways a trial has helped you to better love God, others, or yourself.

In the final column list ways in which the benefits of column four have changed your behavior. The purpose of trials is not just for our own self-worth, but so that we might love others as well. The two greatest commandments are that we love God and that we love one another. So this final column shows how the value we've gained from trials can be used to help others.

You may still doubt that your own trials have any buried treasure, so let's look at some examples. I'll start with my own chart and illustrate how some of my painful experiences have turned into treasures.

WHAT I LIKE ABOUT MYSELF	PAST TRIALS	SUPPORT PEOPLE	BENEFITS FROM TRIALS	LOVE IN ACTION

COLUMN ONE: WHAT I LIKE ABOUT MYSELF

In the first column I wrote that I like my family life, some of my speaking skills, my concern for helping people, the fulfillment I've found in God's love and joy, and the overflow of ministering to others through seminars, books, and films. (This is a very personal list, so if you prefer to keep some things confidential you might want to use a numerical code.)

COLUMN TWO: PAST TRIALS

In the next column, I first wrote down my difficult experience with Bill Gothard. But there are others. For example, I flunked third grade. I've been embarrassed by that for years, and my kids still tease me about it. They wonder how anyone with half a brain could flunk third grade. But now I can smile about it because I've found the treasure in it. Another trial was the time I expected a $2,000 refund on my income taxes, only to learn that I owed $1,700 instead! List whatever *you* consider a trial, even though others may deem it insignificant. (Again, you might want to use some kind of code.)

COLUMN THREE: SUPPORT PEOPLE

During my trials with Bill my feelings were so intense that without the help of some close Christian friends my recovery would have taken much longer. So in column three I list the people God brought into my life to encourage and help me. Over a period of two years, much of that support came in my meetings with the elder Mr. Gothard and through the love of a small group of Christian friends.

COLUMN FOUR: BENEFITS FROM TRIALS

Although extremely painful, I can say now that the benefits of my experience with Bill have been so great that I would go through it again for the gold of love I discovered. Here are a few of the nuggets:

Empathy and Compassion

Because of the pain I felt, I now have tremendous empathy for couples going through a divorce. I understand the agony of separation when the situation is beyond control. My eyes often fill with tears when I listen to a man or woman describe their struggles in a painful relationship. I want so desperately to help them discover what I've learned. Compassion is another important part of love, and it's learned through trials (see 2 Corinthians 1:5–7). I also have a much better understanding of those in midlife crisis, which is very likely what I was experiencing during those two years.

Renewed Appreciation and Love for Norma

Through all my trials, Norma held tightly to me and helped hold our family together.

A Deeper Sense of Love and Forgiveness

When I realized how selfish I had been and yet how my Lord and my family still forgave me, my love and forgiveness for others increased significantly.

Patience

Until my experience with Bill I had always expected things to happen quickly. During this crisis I had no choice but to wait.

Wisdom

I learned what God's priorities for life really are—to love him and to love others!

Love and Acceptance

These have been the greatest benefits of all. My experience with Bill forced me to depend on Christ alone for love and acceptance. I hate to think of how many more years I might have wasted if I had continued to look to Bill or to any other person, thing, or job for fulfillment. Because I was humbled through this experience, I gained the greatest gift—an understanding of God's grace, which gives me the power to love others unconditionally.

Humility and Sensitivity

What about the benefits of flunking third grade? Humility is the most obvious benefit. Not being promoted to fourth grade along with my friends kept me humble for many years. To this day I am self-conscious about my spelling, because my atrocious spelling was one of the reasons I was held back. Even though my spelling has improved, I'm still embarrassed sometimes by words I carelessly misspell. I know, however, that being a better speller will not give me fulfillment. God only gives his grace to the humble. Being humble means I'm weak and in need of God's grace. So whenever embarrassment strikes, I thank God that his grace reflected in my weakness makes me a more loving person.

Flunking third grade also made it difficult for me to read aloud in front of people. One of my most embarrassing moments was being unable to finish reading a portion of Scripture at my church when I was president of a large college group. That experience humbled me and gave me a deep concern for those struggling with dyslexia and other spelling and reading disorders. Also, because I know the pain of being embarrassed, I am extremely careful not to embarrass people who attend my marriage seminars. My embarrassment increased my sensitivity, a requirement for anyone who wants to be a loving person.

Trusting God—the Source of Fulfillment

What about the benefits of owing the Internal Revenue Service $1,700 instead of it owing me $2,000? The first benefit was the reminder that money gives no fulfillment. Although we had to sacrifice to pay the extra money, I knew that neither the money nor anything we could buy with it could add anything to my knowledge of God. Second, we had to trust God to meet our needs. Third, the trial forced me to get professional help and learn to better manage our finances—a benefit that has really paid off over the years.

COLUMN FIVE: LOVE IN ACTION

The treasures I found as a result of my problems with Bill gave me an opportunity to minister around the country. What I learned has been the basis for several books about marriage, two parenting books, a series of cassette tapes, the seminars I teach, a nineteen-part film series, and many counseling opportunities.

The embarrassment of flunking third grade made me more patient with my kids in regard to their schoolwork. Instead of reacting harshly if their grades weren't what I expected, I tried to understand what caused the problem so I could help them succeed. Also, I'm more patient with those who struggle with low self-esteem, no matter what the reason.

I've often used the example of the tax miscalculations to encourage others to go to God alone as their source of life.

I could add many other trials to my list, but I don't want to leave the impression that this concept works only for me. Let's look at how it has worked in the lives of others.

Self-worth Restored

Treasure hunting is important because it builds self-worth. Seventeen-year-old Denise hadn't suffered any experiences as traumatic as Jill's, but constant conflict with her parents was continually reinforcing her poor self-image. Denise challenged me after a seminar, stating that she knew there were *no* benefits in the things she'd endured. "I'm always looking for the first exception," I said to her. "Why don't we sit down and you tell me your problems."

I quickly learned from Denise that she hated four things about her life: She believed she was ugly, stupid, and overweight, and she was convinced her parents were unfair.

"Do you want God's best in your life?" I asked her.

"Yes," she answered.

"What do you think God's best is?"

"I really don't know."

"God's best and highest will is for us to love (value) him with all our hearts and to love (value) others as ourselves. Do you realize that you have everything you need to fulfill God's will and experience God's best in your life?"

"And just how can I find it?" she inquired.

We started with her problems concerning her physical appearance. I asked her if she wanted to be beautiful.

"Of course!" she snapped.

I explained that a humble attitude was the key to physical beauty, because God gives his grace to the humble. I suggested she pray a prayer like this: "Lord, thank you that through love you can give me spiritual beauty that will be reflected in my physical appearance through my eyes and facial expressions. Even though I think I'm unattractive now, thank you that as you teach me how to love you and others, people will begin to see your beauty in me."

Then I suggested that perhaps God was using her appearance to protect her. She seemed puzzled, so I explained further. Because of her appearance, men would not be attracted to her for purely physical reasons, and she would not be tempted to use her appearance to manipulate people. So in any relationship, whether friendship or romance, she would know the person was attracted to her because of her inner, lasting qualities that only God could develop within her.

She smiled for the first time, and her smile revealed a pretty face. I was surprised to see how the simple act of relaxing her facial muscles immediately made her more attractive. When a person can thank God for the good they know is there but cannot yet see, facial expressions often change and others can see a new beauty and a compelling calmness of spirit.

I went on to explain that self-hatred might be the cause of her overeating. If she started to relax and began to like herself, the compulsion to overeat might subside. But even if she could not lose weight, she could still find her fulfillment in God.

Denise's below-average intelligence also held a disguised benefit. Denise had never battled with God over theological issues. For her, a childlike faith came more naturally. Although asking God difficult questions about our faith is not wrong, there is great value in simple faith, as Jesus showed when he used a child as an example of what we must become like in order to enter the kingdom of God (see Luke 18:16).

As we talked, Denise gave evidence that she realized this was true. She told of a number of times when students at her high school had sought her counsel because she was known for being trusting and for having above-average common sense.

We then considered Denise's relationship with her parents. Any support she received from them was based solely on her achievements, which by their standards were few. Denise believed they preferred her brother because he excelled in athletics and earned good grades in school. The concept of unconditional love and affection was foreign to the family. Her father traveled extensively, which Denise resented, and her mother complained about having to raise the kids without his help.

Each of these trials had its benefits. Because Denise felt unloved, her sensitivity to others from similar homes was unusually strong. I explained how that sensitivity could enable her, if she would let it, to reach out to others, to accept them as they are, and to understand their needs. Her parents' favoritism revealed the futility and frustration of expecting people to make her happy. Learning this could lead her into a closer relationship with Jesus, who would never leave her or forsake her. And her father's frequent absences turned out to be the greatest benefit of all. Her need for a father was the major factor that brought her to faith in Jesus. And finally, her poor relationship with her parents could make her more sensitive to her own children if she were to marry at some time in the future.

Denise skipped away from our meeting with a smile on her face. Several years later she sent me a letter detailing what good things God was continuing to do in her life. She had gone on to college, majored in sociology, and become a social worker helping individuals with disabilities. Her trials, she said, produced the patience she needed for this kind of work, so now she too helps people discover treasure in their trials. *The more love she gives, the more her self-worth soars.*

The apostle Paul understood this mystery when he wrote his famous description of love: "Love is patient, love is kind. It does not envy, it does not boast, it is not proud. It is not rude, it is not self-seeking, it is not easily angered, it keeps no record of wrongs. Love does not delight in evil but rejoices with the truth. It always protects, always trusts, always hopes, always perseveres" (1 Corinthians 13:4–7). These qualities of mature love are given to us through trials (see James 1:2; Hebrews 12:10–11).

From Rejection to Acceptance

David was a successful real estate broker when his wife left him and moved with their two young daughters to a city 2,200 miles away. The emotional pain of rejection hurt so badly that David couldn't believe me when I told him we could find a benefit in his trial. We looked at Hebrews 12:11: "No discipline seems pleasant at the time, but painful. Later on, however, it produces a harvest of righteousness and peace for those who have been *trained* by it" (italics added). I explained to him how this trial could, if he was willing, make him more righteous, which meant he would be more Christlike, which meant he would also be more loving.

As we talked further, David realized that his actions had caused his wife to leave him. His priority had been his career rather than his family, so he had ended up neglecting those he loved. David's new priorities were the first benefit of his trial. Next he recognized his self-centeredness and how he had been caught up in reaching for material wealth, which he knew could never give him a fulfilling life. His family wanted *him,* not more of his wealth. This experience forced David to see that no aspect of God's creation could give him lasting satisfaction.

Even though David failed to provide the love his family needed before they moved away, his concern for his daughters was genuine. He wondered how they would adjust to a new city, and particularly how their self-worth would be affected if they did not receive the love they needed. Well, it wasn't too late for him to start expressing his love. This trial showed him that he needed to communicate love to his wife and children. He began to do so in his phone conversations and letters, and he enlisted the help of an older Christian couple to help him learn practical ways of expressing his love. The more he learned about how to love, and the more he actually put that love into action, the more his self-worth improved.

There's a happy ending to this story. It took nearly two years, but his wife did return to a new David.

The Rest of the Story

Let's go back to the story of Jill, where we began the chapter several pages ago. Does treasure hunting really work in a tough situation like that? Here's what we discovered during that day she and her husband visited me in Phoenix.

As we began to look for treasure in her trials, I had to coach her at first, but gradually she began to see the love God had given her through what her family had done out of their own selfishness. She hated to see anyone misused, even on television, and she was extremely sensitive to injustice. Her deep empathy for others helped her raise her daughter. She was very careful about the baby-sitters she selected and was doubly alert to even minor offenses toward her child.

Her sensitivity, which was highly refined because of the verbal abuse she received as a child, made her always careful to not hurt or mislead people with her words. She also had a realistic view of men, which she would apply as she educated her daughter. Even with her husband, who was a very gentle and caring man, she was alert to anything that might be interpreted as child abuse. Her cautiousness helped her husband become a more sensitive and loving mate and father. Jill also had an ability to spot abused women and children simply by the look on their faces. She was very aware of the social problems of incest, spouse abuse, and child abuse.

The greatest benefit she received was her relationship with Jesus Christ. The repeated violation of her body had totally humiliated her and driven her into Jesus' waiting arms. I reminded her that the greater our embarrassment from circumstances beyond our control, the more God's grace is available. "That's true!" she admitted. "Often I've gone running to Christ's arms and found great comfort there." She realized Jesus understood how she felt, for he had been physically and verbally abused and humiliated by his public beating and his execution on a cross. Jill's dependency on Jesus Christ gave her supernatural grace to live and an inner power that many never know.

God transformed Jill's trial into a treasure in a remarkable demonstration of love in action. Her painful past enables her to minister to teenage victims of incest and child abuse in a way few others can. They listen to her because they know she understands them. She emphasizes to the girls their great value, and gradually their self-worth rises as they witness her unconditional love and concern for them. From there she leads them on their own treasure hunt through their trials and on to a loving heavenly Father who gives them a blessing, not a curse.

I compare life to a treasure hunt because I know that in every negative situation God buries a valuable treasure he wants us to have. Sometimes we have to search diligently for it. It may take considerable time. For Monte Johnson, it took several months. But if we search, we *can* find it.

I'm not implying that God causes all trials. I do not believe God was responsible for Jill's repeated sexual abuse by her uncle and brothers. Nor do I believe that God caused David's wife to take their children and desert him or that he caused Denise's parents to verbally and emotionally assault her. Jill, David, and Denise suffered months and years of emotional trauma from these trials until they learned how to treasure hunt. Buried in the debris of their tragedies were benefits as real as rubies and diamonds. As they dug into their tribulations and discovered the gems, their self-worth soared. They once considered themselves worthless; but when they learned the process of turning negatives into positives, they saw the great value they possessed.

The prophet Isaiah saw great treasure as he looked to the coming of Jesus (see Isaiah 61). The Spirit of the Lord was to be with Jesus—"to preach good news to the poor ... to bind up the brokenhearted, to proclaim freedom for the captives and release from darkness for the prisoners ... to comfort all who mourn" (Isaiah 61:1–2). And then look at the treasure promised to all who suffered from various trials: "to bestow on them a crown of beauty instead of ashes, the oil of gladness instead of mourning, and a garment of praise instead of a spirit of despair" (Isaiah 61:3).

The greatest illustration of one who saw the gold in the midst of trial was our Lord Jesus Christ himself. And note the tie to the theme of our book—the theme of joy. In Hebrews 12:2, we're exhorted to fix our eyes on Jesus, the source of life, "the author and perfecter of our faith, who for the *joy* set before him endured the cross, scorning its shame, and sat down at the right hand of the throne of God" (italics added).

Jesus Christ didn't want to go through these trials. He pleaded with his heavenly Father that he would be spared the agony of the cross. Yet, he persevered through it because he knew what was on the other side—the *joy* of our being with him. You and I don't have the advantage of seeing ahead. Often we're in darkness when the storm is raging all around us. But there is a shore over on the other side; there is an end to the trial. And when we find the gold in the trial, we find real joy.

If you are struggling to understand what good can come out of your trials, let me encourage you to write out and memorize some verses. We've mentioned most of them in this chapter: Isaiah 61:3; Romans 8:28–39; 1 Thessalonians 5:16–18; Hebrews 12:9–11; James 1:2; and Romans 5:3–5. Refer to these promises often. Let them sink deep into your heart. Stand in line like the persistent widow of Luke 18 and ask God to make these assurances real for you. Expect God to answer your prayers, for those promises are the "other side" on which he wants you to land.

This truth works for any individual, giving them a genuine sense of value and meaning in life. But for a marriage relationship, when a couple treasure hunts together, it leads to a literal gold mine!

CHAPTER TEN

We're in This Trial Together!

AL AND JO RECENTLY had a very stressful week. It started when a friend and her daughter moved to town, and Al and Jo agreed to help them move into their new home. While starting to unload the truck, a dolly fell on top of the daughter, slicing her hand. Jo drove the two newcomers to the hospital emergency room, where the girl was X-rayed and received five stitches. Meanwhile, Al and crew tried to figure out where to put all of the boxes and furniture.

A couple of days later, school started. The first day, Al and Jo's son Jonathan learned that his best friend's older brother (only nineteen years old) had just been killed in a climbing accident. Another classmate of both Jonathan and his older brother, Joshua, was dealing with the imminent death of his father from cancer. Those are sobering moments for young teenagers. Add to that a very heavy class load that left Joshua feeling overwhelmed. And Al and Jo's youngest daughter, Anna, managed to go to school, but she was feeling sick and needed to go to the doctor.

Meanwhile, Al was trying to meet his deadline on this book and Jo was working hard to meet a deadline on her book—then suddenly a major crisis erupted at Al's day job, completely changing his schedule and plans. That week, one former employee moved away, and another new employee decided to change plans, leaving Al's already shorthanded team in shock. By the end of the week, both Al and Jo were exhausted from the stress of the emotional roller coaster the family had endured.

It's times like this that can strain a marriage. Or it can draw a couple closer together. The one thing you can't change is the fact that life happens, and we all will live through intense periods when everything seems to be rushing at us at once. You may wonder, *Can there be joy in the midst of these trying times?* Absolutely! Finding that joy as a couple is one of the most rewarding things you can do.

After reading the previous chapter on treasure hunting, some may be saying, "That's fine for you, but you don't know my problems. Surely there can't be *any* treasure in my situation."

Are there exceptions to this principle? After counseling with hundreds of individuals, I have yet to find a single one. Sometimes we have to dig deep, but the treasure is always there. Sometimes the treasure is coated with corrosion, but if we do some scraping we begin to see its value. And a glimpse of the first sparkle of gold keeps us scraping until the shiny nugget is free from its ugly coating.

I've found at least three scrapers that prepare us to discover treasure in trials. The first is *taking time to grieve.* Complete healing usually requires a grieving process. Immediately after a tragedy, the victim needs comfort from loving, sensitive people. Regret usually sets in next, followed by denial and an attempt to minimize the tragedy. Finally, after weeks or months, comes the willingness to treasure hunt. Although we *can* begin to treasure hunt immediately after a trial, and sometimes even during a trial, most of us need time to regain our strength before we begin the emotionally draining digging process.

The second scraper is *faith*. Faith adds muscle to the scraping process, even in the worst of trials. Faith is knowing God's will, and it is God's will that we find treasure in trials. Faith is fixing our eyes on Jesus, "the author and perfecter of our faith" (Hebrews 12:2) who showed us what faith looks like in the ultimate trial, the cross. He endured the cross "for the joy set before him." We can endure our trial because there is treasure at the other end.

The third scraper—*thanksgiving*—is closely related to the second. Thanksgiving expresses our faith that God will indeed bring treasure out of our trials by producing love in us.

Let me emphasize again that although good can come out of tragedy, we need not conclude that tragic situations are good. As Paul said in Romans 6, God's grace is applied to our sin, but we do not sin so that grace may increase. Woe to the man who would rape or abuse anyone (see Luke 17:1)—but when an evil act is committed against us, God's love *is* available for healing and growth.

One of the greatest forums for treasure hunting is within a committed marriage relationship. While it works wonders for any individual, when a couple can treasure hunt together with regard to the trials of life, they will find themselves living in a gold mine.

Biblical Examples of Treasure Hunting

Scripture abounds with examples of good coming out of evil situations. We shudder at the injustice meted out to Jacob's son, Joseph. Out of jealousy, his brothers sold him into slavery. Then, after he had risen to prominence in Potiphar's household, he was unjustly accused by Potiphar's wife and thrown into prison. But many years later Joseph was able to say to his repentant brothers, "*You intended to harm me, but God intended it for good* to accomplish what is now being done, the saving of many lives" (Genesis 50:20, italics added).

David was another victim of jealousy. King Saul, on hearing that David was to replace him as king, set out to destroy him and foil God's plan. Enraged, insane, and jealous, the king hunted his onetime friend and counselor for years through the desert (see 1 Samuel 19–24). The experience, though bitter at the time, made David a better king.

Peter, although humiliated when he denied three times that he knew Jesus (see Matthew 26:69–75), turned that distasteful experience into a powerful treasure that enabled him to follow Jesus' command to "feed my sheep" (John 21:17).

This was true for couples as well. Take Zechariah and Elizabeth, who suffered because they never had children and were now an elderly couple. Infertility is a painful experience for many couples, and it was even more so in those days, for barrenness was interpreted as a lack of God's blessing. Yet this couple faithfully continued to serve the Lord in the midst of their pain.

Luke tells the story of how Zechariah and Elizabeth finally learned how good God is. Their pain led to a special call, the birth of a son who would be known as John the Baptist (see Luke 1:57–66), the one who would pave the way for arrival of the Messiah—Jesus Christ. Was the trial worth it? Zechariah and Elizabeth would say, "Absolutely!"

A negative example can also show what is lost when a couple *can't* treasure hunt together. Take the case of Job, whose life we all associate with intense suffering. When his trials were over, he still didn't understand why he had suffered what he suffered, but he did gain immense treasure—he had an audience with God, and God honored him for his faithfulness (see Job 42:10–17).

What about Job's wife. The only reference we have to her was her advice to Job to "curse God and die" (Job 2:9). Not very encouraging, to be sure! She couldn't see past the calamities that had befallen them. There is no further record of her participating in the discussions or in the blessings God bestowed after the ordeal was over. I submit that Job's wife was the loser as a result.

The Scriptures can provide us with the tools we need to seek gold. Let's look at just two examples. The author of Hebrews writes, "Moreover, we have all had human fathers who disciplined us and we respected them for it. How much more should we submit to the Father of our spirits and live! . . . No discipline seems pleasant at the time, but painful. Later on, however, it produces a harvest of righteousness and peace for those who have been trained by it" (Hebrews 12:9, 11).

Is it possible that your trial is being used by God to discipline you? I can certainly say this was part of what God was doing in my life some twenty years ago. My life was out of balance, and God needed to correct that. Is there something in your life that needs correction? If so, what? If discipline produces a harvest of righteousness and peace, can you see any righteousness coming from it? If not, note those words *later on*—perhaps you are too close to the trial right now. If you are right in the midst of suffering, it may be hard to see the harvest. But at least you can claim it, believing that God *will* produce righteousness and peace for you.

Here's another example from Paul's letter to the Romans: "We also rejoice in our sufferings, because we know that suffering produces perseverance; perseverance, character; and character, hope. And hope does not disappoint us, because God has poured out his love into our hearts by the Holy Spirit, whom he has given us" (Romans 5:3–5).

There are lots of possibilities here. You might ask yourself questions like, "How is my trial producing perseverance?" "Can I identify an aspect of my character that's being strengthened in my trial?" "Can I see any future good that might come out of this trial?" (Seeing a future good is *hope*—and hope doesn't disappoint us.)

The last sentence of this passage is incredible! Think about these words: "God has *poured out his love* into our hearts." Ask yourself how God has poured love into your heart during your trial. Do you feel more love for God? How about more love for others? If you don't feel love right now, who is responsible for giving you that love? (That's right—*you* don't manufacture it. It's given to you by the *Holy Spirit.*)

There are so many Bible passages we could examine in our search for gold. But you can do it yourself. Read the Gospels and the Letters. Read the book of Psalms. And as you read, search for gold. Pray as you read: "God, is this my treasure? Show me the gold."

Treasure Hunting as a Couple

The first thing Al and Jo did after their stressful week was to schedule a time to be together, just the two of them. That meant coffee and pastry at a favorite French restaurant. There they connected, telling each other how they were feeling—tired, stressed, overwhelmed. But this was much more than a venting session, for it also was a time of seeking God's good in the middle of the trials. What they did was a variation of what we examined in the last chapter.

Let's take the five columns we used in the last chapter and revise them for a marriage context. Al and Jo had a pad of paper and wrote down answers to five questions. First, they asked what they liked about their marriage. Second, they identified the trials they were going through. Third, they talked about what friends were available to give them support. Fourth, they searched for the benefit in their trials. Finally, they talked about putting love into action, answering, "How can we use what we've learned this week in order to help others?"

Why is this so important for a couple? For one thing it changes the tone of our discussions. A fulfilled couple seeks to find treasure in the trials of life instead of laying blame on others. As we saw a couple of chapters ago, pride wants to blame others for all of our problems. Treasure hunting seeks to find the good God wants to bring out of the trials. It's really a practice of *grace.* As Jo says, "Treasure hunting beats the blame game."

WHAT WE LIKE ABOUT OUR MARRIAGE	PAST TRIALS	SUPPORT PEOPLE	BENEFITS FROM TRIALS	LOVE IN ACTION

Let's look at how Al and Jo worked through the process of their intensely stressful week. First, they reviewed some of the things they appreciate about their marriage. This is a habit they have developed—they like to concentrate on what is good about each other and their relationship. These are some of the things they noted:

- We don't punish each other for our mistakes.
- We don't hold grudges.
- We have fun together and laugh a lot—and there's lots to laugh about.
- We've been through a lot, and each trial has made us stronger.
- We appreciate our differences, so we accept each other as we are, and we haven't tried to change each other.
- We're the proud parents of three wonderful children.
- We try and connect daily, even when we're apart.

You get the idea. There are a lot of things Al and Jo find to celebrate in their relationship, and that's a wonderful foundation for treasure hunting.

Second, they identified the issues and events of the week that caused their stress. While each issue was a challenge, they agreed that, when combined, it was far more than the usual things of life. Moreover, all of these were events or circumstances outside of their control. There was no way to change the facts. They could run from them, but that wouldn't help. At least they could face it all together.

Third, they talked about their support group. This is a critical component, for life is not meant to be lived in isolation. Norma and I have, for years, been part of a group of couples that meets regularly to help each other in our marriages. We also have what we call a "911 group"—a couple or two we can call, or they can call us, at any time to get help when we're in over our heads.

When Al and Jo moved to Colorado Springs, this was one of the more challenging areas, for it takes a while to gain that support group. Fortunately, after eight years, that's no longer a problem. They named two couples they could call instantly if they needed to. But right now, they didn't need help in their marriage, but rather they needed encouragement from friends. Jo could get that with a group of mothers with whom she prayed each week at school. Al had a couple of men he connected with by phone, telling them the circumstances and asking for prayer.

But Al also felt he needed more this time. So he called a friend of twenty-seven years who is in the same line of work. They live two hours apart, and whenever one or the other needs a friend, they meet in the middle—at a restaurant in Denver. Two days after he called, Al and his friend spent three hours talking. Al was able to talk through all the issues he was facing at work, get some valuable counsel, and be assured his friend would be praying for him in the coming days.

Don't underestimate the power of good friends in a marriage. In a healthy marriage relationship, the wife has strong women friends, the husband has several strong male friends, and the couple also has other couples with whom they enjoy spending time together.

So what are some of the benefits Al and Jo found from this stressful week? This is the fourth question in the chart, and they wrote down several things:

- This week makes other weeks look very good, reminding us to thank God for our everyday blessings.
- Making it through this week means we can make it through other trials.
- Regarding our son Joshua, we completely empathize with the pressure he's experiencing at school, for we have similar pressure.
- We know God is in control, and there are several opportunities to watch him work.
- Regarding Al's work, we realize he has no choice but to trust God, and so as God works, our faith will grow.
- We have sensed God's presence and comfort throughout the week, reminding us that *God* is the source of life—not people, circumstances, things, or career.

- Joshua's heavy load is another piece in the building of his godly character, and while it's hard, he's responding wonderfully. This test will make him a stronger man.
- Our circumstances aren't nearly as hard as those two families at school, one who lost a loved one, the other facing the impending loss of a loved one.

The fifth area is love in action—using the good we've found in our trials to love others. Al and Jo thought of others who might need encouragement, starting with the two families at school. In addition, this was a time to help their sons learn how to minister to hurting friends. They coached Jonathan in how to be sensitive to his friend's moods and emotions, and to provide extra opportunity for that friend to talk or just to do some things together. Al and Jo thought about the two people who had left his department, about their hurts and needs. That motivated them to spend extra time in prayer. It also caused them to be more sensitive to other friends or families who may be facing similar kinds of pressures at work. Regarding Joshua's heavy workload, Jo committed to spending time with him each day to coach him and encourage him to get through his homework assignments.

Do you see what they're doing? You can do this as a couple in small trials as well as in large. I say again, to hunt for the treasure will bring you wonderfully together as a couple.

My wife, Norma, has learned over the years to go straight to the Lord at the first hint of a trial. She seeks the Lord, and I seek the Lord. I know she's taken care of by Christ, and she knows I'm taken care of by Christ. Thus, we're comfortable in our relationship. When there's a trial, Norma says, "I make myself thank God, and immediately I try to see one or two benefits."

One of the trials that brought Norma and I closer together was the birth of our granddaughter, Hannah. I was on a trip promoting a book when Kari was hospitalized. For the last three months of her pregnancy, she would have to be flat on her back. This was her third pregnancy; she had lost her second baby a year before at nineteen weeks. The doctors told her that staying in bed was her only hope of saving this child.

This was a traumatic experience for our daughter, who'd never suffered so much as a broken bone in her life. Norma went to the hospital daily to minister to Kari. Kari had heard us teach and use the truths from this book—that our life comes from God, not circumstances, and that there is great value in treasure hunting in our trials. Norma prayed daily with Kari and helped her apply these truths.

Then each night Norma would come home to an empty house. I was out on a long book tour and couldn't get home except on weekends. Both of us were emotionally hurting. Norma had to stay positive for Kari's benefit but felt very weak inside. I was upset that I couldn't be there to help, though there was little I could do. Still, I wanted to be home with my wife and daughter.

What treasure did we gain from this trial? First, we realized we couldn't rush the process. Kari's hospitalization brought back the trauma of her previous miscarriage. Norma and Kari understood there was a very real possibility they might never hold this baby. That caused them to grieve again the loss of the first baby, something that needed to be done.

Of course, when everything went well with Hannah's birth, the sorrow was quickly forgotten. She brings us immense joy. As her grandfather, my heart melts at anything she does. Anything she asks me for—well, I simply can't resist! Kari gained deeper empathy through the trial. She goes back to the hospital often to visit and encourage people who are hospitalized for long periods of time. And she and Hannah promote the ministry of the local Ronald McDonald House, where families can stay overnight when their child is in the hospital.

Treasure Hunting Can Work in Any Marriage

Does treasure hunting work in every situation? Let's return to the stories told in chapter 1—the Bramletts and the Mitchells. If these couples were to fill out a chart like the one we've created, what might it look like? I'm sure they could give many details, but let's make a start on each. First the Bramletts:

What did the Bramletts like about their marriage? Well, honestly, the first years there wasn't much to like. John seemed more in love with football and alcohol than with his wife. Nancy felt neglected and abused. But there were some things she *could* be thankful for. John was a hard worker and had provided well for her financially. They had two wonderful children. And Nancy's commitment to stick with the marriage when many others would have dashed toward divorce gave the relationship a chance to change.

The trials were easy to identify. There was no closeness between John and Nancy. John was involved with other women. He was on the verge of becoming an alcoholic. And when drunk, he was abusive to Nancy.

As far as support, there wasn't a whole lot until Nancy began going to church and becoming involved in a women's Bible study. There, she found a group of women to whom she could express her pain and who would pray for her. What's more, it was the church body that eventually led to John's conversion, particularly the visit of the two deacons to their home.

What good could you find in the trials of this marriage? The first, most obvious one, is that each found life to be empty, and their needs drove them into the arms of Jesus Christ. Their lives radically changed as a result. John became a loving husband and father. They found that Jesus more than met their needs, even when they weren't as financially well-off as before. Their lives declare the message that there are no hopeless cases. God can change *any* individual, even John Bramlett. God can revive *any* marriage, even one that seemed to be hopelessly dead, like John and Nancy's.

Love in action is the exciting thing for this couple. They now have a full-time ministry to people. Because of John's National Football League experience, he's had opportunity to give his testimony around the country, and thousands have been touched by his message. Nancy leads Bible studies with women and finds numerous opportunities to minister to women in abusive relationships like the one she once had. Most of all, their marriage is a shining testimony to couples who are struggling.

The situation of the Mitchells is quite different. They were Christians who were committed to their marriage, involved in church, and successful in their community. In many ways, they had a model relationship. There was much to like about their marriage.

But the phone call to Bo from the FBI changed their circumstances, and going to prison was a shattering experience. Bo felt humiliated. Gari struggled with depression. The children were confused about God and his goodness. Gari says that "it felt like I'd been hit with a tidal wave."

For support, the couple had a dear friend named Helen Dye. Helen wasn't afraid to confront Bo with the truth—that he was totally consumed by his business and was neglecting his children. There were also many friends from church who came alongside to encourage them.

What is the treasure they found in this trial? It started with Gari telling her husband that this situation "will be the salvation of your children." This was one of only two times in her life when she felt God clearly speaking to her. But initially she didn't know what that meant: "As we walked out of the courtroom after Bo's sentencing, Ashley was hysterical, and Andy was mad." During the 137 days Bo was in prison, Ashley wrote him more than a hundred letters. In one, she said, "I just want you to know, Dad, that what Mom heard from God that day has happened in my life."

Andy struggled the most, but he, too, found treasure. Bo still gets choked up thinking about one special moment that took their relationship to a deeper level: "The inmates were always talking about how to get furloughs to spend a day or two with family. It was all talk—I never actually saw such a furlough granted. One day, my son asked a guard about how he might obtain a furlough to come *into* the prison and spend a night with me. The guard thought he was crazy—no one had ever asked to come voluntarily and stay inside the prison. But that's how important our relationship had become."

The love of Bo's family was actually a powerful ministry to the inmates. During Bo's confinement, there were ninety-seven days that he was allowed to have members of his family visit him. His family actually came on ninety-five of those occasions—a tremendous witness to the inmates, many of whom had never experienced a truly functional family.

For Bo personally, this trial forced him to be quiet and seek God for the first time in his life. The time in prison amounted to an extended retreat, and what he discovered shocked him. He realized he was expecting money and people and career to provide what only God could provide. For the first time, he truly let God be his life. "I got to see what it's supposed to look like with Christ," he says. He spent more time reading the Bible and praying than ever before. He realized he had been neglecting his family, and his priorities changed. So Bo and Gari benefited to the extent that when Bo left prison, he was much more of the husband Gari needed and the father their children needed.

Let's see what happened as this couple put their love in action. Today, Bo is no longer dominated by business. While in prison, Bo heard a song that expressed his feelings—"Learning to Live Again" by Garth Brooks. Bo was introduced to the famous entertainer, and they became close friends, in part because of Bo's experience. In time, they formed a foundation for kids called "Touch Them All." Bo serves as president; working with professional athletes, the foundation raised approximately $3,000,000 in its first year to help meet health and educational needs of inner-city kids.

There have been other methods of outreach as well. Bo and Gari were able to tell their story on the Focus on the Family radio broadcast, which helped thousands of other individuals and couples who are going through trials. Bo declared that "the circumstances of a Christian's life are ordained by God. In the life of a Christian, there's no such thing as chance. God, by his providence, brings you into circumstances you cannot understand, but the Spirit of God understands."

We could look at many more examples of people who have found treasure in their hurts and sufferings. Perhaps you're going through a problem right now and you can't find any treasure. Work through your own chart. If you still can't find it, thank God that *it is there* even though you don't see it yet. In fact, thanksgiving is one of the best ways to discover the benefits of a trial, because it expresses our faith in God's promise that good can be found in all our sufferings.

Faith is trusting that God's Word is reliable. If God promises, "We are going over to the other side," then we *are* going over to the other side. Many promises in Scripture can sustain us in our trials. They are the equivalent of Jesus' promise to the disciples (see Mark 4:35).

You may be getting the impression that we can only learn to love through trials. Not true. We can often short-circuit trials by humbling ourselves. Jesus proclaimed, "For whoever exalts himself will be humbled, and whoever humbles himself will be exalted" (Matthew 23:12). One reason the genuinely humble are lifted up is because God honors those who love. I prefer to humble myself and avoid trials and discipline whenever possible. Avoiding trials completely, however, is impossible.

No one likes trials, yet no one can escape them. We can let them ruin our lives—making us bitter, angry, and resentful—or we can look for the treasure that will let us love and serve others.

By allowing trials to draw us to God, our batteries will not only be charged but will be on the brink of overflow—the continual experience of those who know and carry out the greatest commandments: love God and love others.

CHAPTER ELEVEN

Gaining a Clear Purpose in Life

THE ROUTINE WAS EXHILARATING, like that of a rock and roll star. We traveled in a special bus from city to city. Each night I'd speak twice in a (hopefully) packed concert hall. After the show, copies of my latest book, *Making Love Last Forever*, were sold. Then we'd climb back on the bus, and I'd eat a bowl of cereal and retire to the master suite in the back while the rest of the team slept in bunks. The next morning, we'd wake up in another city. I'd go for a run, do some promotion, and present another show. It was a lot of fun!

Naturally, I shared all of this excitement with Norma—by phone. She had decided she had to stay home and continue to run the office. There were future seminars to be arranged, a staff that needed her, and a home to maintain. What I didn't realize was that all of the media attention I was enjoying was causing a huge increase in phone calls at the office.

With a month left on the tour, the company organizing the events asked if I would do a second thirty-city tour in the spring.

I flew home for a break and quickly wrote up a four-page proposal for Norma and the ministry directors. At our staff meeting, I raised the question. Norma was unusually quiet during the first part of the discussion. Finally, someone asked what she was thinking. She held up the proposal and said, "I'm not sure whether you should do this or not, but this proposal feels like divorce papers."

Thinking she was joking, I laughed and said, "Yeah, right. Divorce papers! I want to continue this tour for *Making Love Last Forever.* It's a tremendous opportunity to minister to a lot of people!"

Norma didn't smile but calmly said, "You're not listening. This has been very hard on our staff. It's quadrupled the pressure we're under. You have no idea how much work this is— the pressure of connecting you with all these radio and television stations. I don't think any of us could take another thirty-city tour. I'm not sure our marriage could take another thirty-city tour."

Norma had my attention now. I had no idea how much stress this was causing. "Are you really serious about divorce?"

"No, it's not divorce," she answered. "But if you did this tour, it would be *like* a divorce, because you would be gone so much and you'd be married to your traveling team."

One last time I checked to see what the others thought. "How do the rest of you feel about this?" I asked. Of course, Norma signs their paychecks, not me. So they wisely voted, unanimously, against another tour. I had to go back to the company and tell them the answer was no. They didn't like the answer and put a lot of pressure on me to sign up for the second tour. But the decision was final. When Norma said "no," I would not waver— because she is so valuable to me, and our marriage relationship is so valuable. How could I possibly go and speak to other people's wives while I was undermining my own?

There was a time when I might have plunged ahead in a ministry venture, regardless of whether my wife was supportive.

I've learned that such an attitude is contrary to how God works. In serving people, God's will is never fulfilled at the expense of our spouse and loved ones. So how *do* we keep God's will clear?

What Is God's Will for Us?

God's Word addresses this question directly. In fact, Scripture specifically states God's will for each of us. The power of this truth motivates and energizes us and adds creativity and excitement to a marriage. It can draw us out of bed in the morning with renewed enthusiasm. It tells us when we're in the center of God's will, gives us a sense of purpose, and adds to our self-worth.

So what is God's will? A lawyer once asked Jesus that same question. Jesus told him that God's highest will, the greatest commandment, was to "love the Lord your God with all your heart and with all your soul and with all your mind" (Matthew 22:37). Then he added the second greatest commandment: "Love your neighbor as yourself" (Matthew 22:39). That pretty well covers it all; everything else required by God flows from these two commandments.

Obedience to the first commandment energizes us; obedience to the second makes us overflow with motivation, creativity, and excitement about life.

Seeing people renewed, healed, blessed, encouraged, and motivated by our love for them increases our self-worth—and that starts the overflow in our lives.

People frequently ask me how to find God's specific will about such things as who they should marry, what vocation they should pursue, and whether or not they should change jobs or careers. For years I had similar questions. Since 1978, however, I've known God's will for me, and I have eagerly watched it materialize.

I believe God has something for each of us to accomplish. I've simplified the process of understanding and practicing God's will with a system I call *The FIVE Ms.* If you or someone you know wants to "nail down" God's will, this simple five-point plan might help. Picture a circle with the word *Master* in the center. The words *Mission, Method, Maintenance,* and *Mate* surround it like four points on a compass.

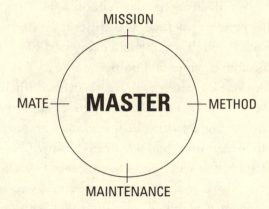

The five *M*s illustrate both elements of God's will—loving God and loving others—by asking five questions.

- *Master* asks, "Who am I going to live for?"
- *Mission* asks, "What does God want me to do?"
- *Method* asks, "How will I fulfill my mission?"
- *Maintenance* asks, "How will I evaluate and adjust my methods?"
- *Mate* asks, "Do we agree about our mission and methods?"

Notice that *Master* is the first and most important aspect of God's will. The other four elements relate to God's second command. When all five parts work in harmony, we experience the overflowing life promised to those who are in the center of God's will.

This has been the model for Al and Jo in their twenty-two-plus years of marriage. On their very first date, they established that their Master was Jesus Christ, and throughout the years they have striven to please him.

Al and Jo also shared a common mission—to be God's instruments to enrich the lives of others by leading them into relationship with God and helping them grow into mature disciples.

Jo's method—in fact her desire since she was a little girl—was to teach elementary-age students. When Al met her, Jo was teaching fifth grade in a Christian school. Al also enjoyed teaching, but his primary method was different—he felt called to communicate through writing and being part of creative teams that produced magazines and books.

Over the years, their mission has remained unchanged, but their methods have changed several times. For two years, they talked about starting a writing business, and they agreed to do so about the time their first child was born. Meanwhile, Jo felt called to stop teaching after eight years to concentrate on her children. For six years, Al and Jo ran a business where Al wrote and edited for various clients (including me). But then, both sensed it was time for another change, which led to Al working in a corporate environment. No longer was he just involved in writing, but his ministry expanded as he worked with other writers and editors.

As their kids grew older, Jo's methods changed as well. After homeschooling her children for a few years, she became more of an encourager as they attended a Christian school, and she supported the teachers by assisting in the classroom and praying for them as part of a "Moms In Touch" group. For one year, she tried going back to work as a teacher, but it no longer felt right. Then an opportunity came for her to write—another way of using her gift of teaching. To date, she's coauthored two books—*Decorating on a Shoestring* and *Dressing Your Family on a Shoestring*—while staying at home and continuing to be a mother to their three children.

Al and Jo talk frequently about their methods for fulfilling their mission in life, and they feel God is preparing them for another chapter that may involve international work. They don't know when it may happen—it could be years away. But it influenced their decision to buy a smaller home, simplify their lifestyle, and get completely out of debt so they're ready to act if and when God chooses to move them. Until then, they get in line, pray, and wait to see what God has in store for them while continuing the work he's given them to do.

This example shows all five points in action—a husband and wife enjoying life and ministry together. There is immense joy when a couple can do that. Let's explore each of the five areas in greater depth.

Master—Who Am I Living for?

The first *M* asks if I am living for my own self-centered desires, or for God. We reflected on this in the first eight chapters. Acknowledging God as the source of my life means that I treasure God and his ways above all else. Phrased as a prayer it says: "God, I love you. I commit my life to you one hundred percent. I understand that your highest will for me is to love you and to love others as I love myself. You said that if we obey these commandments, we are fulfilling all the laws of Scripture (Matthew 22:40). I am committed to doing that, no matter what it takes."

New Testament writers agree that loving God and loving others are the highest commandments, the royal decree, the law of God. Paul declares that one word—love—sums up the entire law (Galatians 5:14). John says we prove our love for God by loving others (1 John 4:7–8). And James says we do right if we really keep the royal law, "Love your neighbor as yourself" (James 2:8).

A basic principle about my own life can be summed up in one sentence: I realize I'm a "10" to God, but I choose to value God and others higher than I do myself (see Philippians 2:3–4). The highest position I can ever attain is to be a *servant* to God and others.

In the last chapter, we saw how God buries treasures in our trials. Through persistent digging we can find the gems of love, but using them for our own fulfillment and satisfaction is only part of the plan; the second half of God's law requires us to *invest* our newfound treasure in the lives of others.

Mission—What Does God Want Me to Do?

Since God is our master, asking him what he wants us to do in regard to loving people starts the process that uncovers our basic purpose for living. While Jesus Christ fills us, we are to search for ways to express his love to others, which is what it means to discover our mission.

Learning what people need and then looking for creative ways to meet those needs unlock the door to all successful relationships and enterprises. Those who learn the secret of serving people's real needs are the most successful. We can take this principle much deeper, however. Many people succeed in serving others, but predominantly for self-centered motives. We've already examined the futility of such efforts. Genuine fulfillment comes only through knowing and loving God first and then through serving others in response to God's love.

It took two years to learn God's specific purpose for me after I stopped working for Bill Gothard. I used this four-point checklist to determine my mission in life.

I CONSULTED SCRIPTURE

As I read the Bible, passages about relationships jumped out at me as though God was drawing my attention to them. In Isaiah 58 I read phrases like "to set the oppressed free" and to "break every yoke" (Isaiah 58:6). The words "rebuild the ancient ruins" (Isaiah 58:12) made me think immediately of how Jesus could rebuild ruined families. I used this passage as a basis for many hours of prayer.

When I read Luke 4, where Jesus said he was the fulfillment of the prophecy in Isaiah 61, my heart leaped: "The Spirit of the Lord is on me, because he has anointed me to preach good news to the poor. He has sent me to proclaim freedom for the prisoners and recovery of sight for the blind, to release the oppressed" (Luke 4:18). The words *freedom* and *release* caught my attention. The Greek words from which they are translated are the basis of the word *forgiveness,* which means to untie someone so he or she can be restored. That's exactly what I wanted to do—untie people from the knots that kept them from experiencing full and meaningful relationships.

I proceeded carefully in this process because I do not advocate pointing to isolated verses and stating, "This is God's verse for me." I went further by seeking God and waiting for his peace after I had checked as many facts in Scripture as possible.

While studying Scripture I also kept my eyes open to the world around me and saw that some of society's greatest needs were in the area of family relationships. Experts confirmed my observations. Over and over they testified that family deterioration was one of the major problems in the United States and around the world.

I PRAYED THAT I WOULD HAVE GOD'S DESIRES

God has promised to give us the desires of our heart if we delight in him (see Psalm 37:4). As I read passages about relationships I prayed, "Lord, is this your heartbeat? Is this what you want me to do? I only want to follow your plan."

As I prayed, read Scripture, and heard about the thousands of crumbling family relationships, I began to sense how God felt about this problem. With that understanding came a desire to do something about it.

I SOUGHT THE COUNSEL OF FRIENDS

In addition to searching Scripture and praying, I quizzed others about what they imagined me doing for the rest of my life. I encouraged them to not limit their thinking to what they already knew about my knowledge and skills. Norma immediately responded by saying, "I see you doing something different than what you're doing today." Even while I was still working with Bill Gothard, she often told me she didn't think I was in the right spot because I was doing more administration than counseling, and she strongly believed that counseling and speaking were my strengths. I'm ashamed to admit I ignored her input for many years.

One day a close friend stopped by my house to say he had been praying for me. He knew of my struggle to determine God's plan as to how I could demonstrate God's love for people. When he said he felt impressed to read Isaiah 58 to me, I felt my eyes open wide. Of all the Scriptures he could have selected! "I see you releasing oppressed families and breaking every yoke that binds families in disharmony." Then he added, "I know this passage doesn't refer specifically to you, but when I read it I saw you jetting around the world, strengthened by the Lord with the heritage of Jacob."

Eventually all who knew me well reinforced what I was already learning from Scripture. Then one day my close friend Jim Stewart, a real estate broker and developer, drove me around town to see the various lots he was developing. As we rode, I summarized what I felt God was leading me to do.

"I've been praying about you and how I can help families through what I do," Jim said. "Much of my time is spent developing and selling commercial and residential buildings, so maybe what I can do is to help finance your work."

When our church personnel committee met to consider my future, their enthusiasm compounded my own. They even wanted to ask the church to help finance my mission. And so it went. Person after person corroborated what I sensed God was calling me to do.

Checking with all these people confirmed to me that my goal was not selfish, that I was not simply being anxious about personal gain or loss. My relationship with Jesus Christ met all my needs for personal worth and achievement, so I prayed, "Lord, I'm already satisfied with you—you are filling my life. Now show me what you want me to do for others." Although I trusted God to reveal his plan in his time, the number of lives splintering around me challenged my patience with a sense of urgency. So I kept saying, "Hurry up, Lord. But take your time."

I TESTED MY PEACE

A fourth test of knowing God's mission was gauging his peace in my heart. When I was nearly certain that my desires matched what God wanted me to do, I thanked him that he would be faithful to answer my request. I stood in his prayer line each day, knowing he would reveal his specific will for me. Then I waited for the peace of God that transcends all understanding (Philippians 4:7), which I knew would guard my heart and mind in the Lord and keep me from doubting, fretting, or continually questioning.

Sometimes I pretended I was teaching at a conference. As I did, I examined myself to see if I had peace about it. Or I envisioned myself working in a counseling center, going through a whole week of appointments. What types of people would I see? Depressed and despairing parents? Misunderstood husbands and wives? Lonely singles? When I imagined myself helping husbands and wives find restoration with the Lord and harmony with each other, I had tremendous peace and excitement.

Finally I knew my mission: to mend broken relationships between people and between people and God. Specifically, I committed myself to love God and my family first, and on the basis of those relationships to teach others what I was learning and to help them discover their own mission and method. Today my mission statement is "to enthusiastically motivate others to highly value God, others, and themselves."

Unfortunately, many people make crucial decisions about the next step, the *method,* which includes education and career, without pausing to determine their mission. I believe this is one reason for the proliferation of midlife crises. It may also be a reason some people don't finish their education. College is a method, and a college education has much more value if we know our mission.

Method—How Will I Fulfill My Mission?

Some people enjoy seeking God's will but hesitate to move when he reveals it. Knowing our mission, although an imperative first step, is only the beginning. After testing it to be sure it's right, we need to move through open doors to fulfill it. First, we need to evaluate the variety of possible methods to accomplish our mission. Here are some examples of missions and methods:

MISSION (What I'll do in life)	METHOD (How I'll do it)	
Relieve people of physical pain	Doctor Dentist Nurse Physical therapist	Hospital administrator Pharmacist Relief worker
Feed those who are hungry	Restaurant (owner or worker) Missionary Grocery store (owner or worker) World hunger relief	
Provide shelter for people	Building contractor Remodeler Interior decorator Motel operator Builder of inexpensive homes for poor	
Reach the unreached for Christ	Missionary Airplane pilot Preacher Tract writer	Crusade team member Film producer Evangelist

This is where the fun and the adventure really begin. Part of the enjoyment of pursuing various methods is realizing that our natural abilities are not the only criteria for determining whether or not to use a particular method. With enough study, time, and experience, and by drawing on the power of the Holy Spirit, we can excel in almost any field.

Suppose a woman's mission is to relieve people of physical pain. She could do a variety of things to accomplish her mission: Become a medical doctor or dentist; work for the Red Cross; raise money to send medical teams to third-world countries; do research to discover new pain-relieving drugs; become a paramedic, a nurse, or a physical therapist; and so forth.

To carry out my mission of strengthening relationships I had an unlimited number of methods to choose from. I could teach seminars, counsel, become a pastor, disciple couples, become a psychologist or a social worker, serve as a chaplain in a hospital, and so forth.

The process of eliminating methods is as difficult as thinking of them. One thing I did (which, incidentally, I continue to do to try to keep my skills sharp) was to ask experts how they thought I could accomplish my mission. For example, I talked with successful writers to learn what makes some books better than others; I studied popular speakers to learn what makes them effective; and I read books and periodicals to stay current on the latest insights in counseling. Throughout this process I tried not to rush God, but I didn't want to wait any longer than necessary to begin fulfilling his call.

Christian psychologist Dr. Henry Brandt strongly influenced my choice of methods. In 1978, while teaching at a conference with him in the Virgin Islands, I told him what I believed God wanted me to do, and he gave me this fantastic advice: "Gary," he said, "I've used a lot of methods to help couples in my thirty years of ministry, and I've concluded that five of them are the best for ministering to people who are in difficult relationships. The first one helps the most people. The others follow in descending order of effectiveness."

1. Write a book. This method scared me. How could someone who has difficulty in spelling ever write a book. But Dr. Brandt was emphatic. "You'll help more people more effectively by forcing yourself to clarify your message through the printed word," he noted. "And you'll help people you'd never meet otherwise."

2. Record my messages on tape. This method offered a little more hope. By refining my messages and recording them on audiocassettes I could make them available all over the world.

3. Record my refined messages on film or videotape. The more specialized my message became, the more strongly Dr. Brandt felt about my need to investigate this possibility. Initially I sensed that this, too, was something I could never do.

4. Speak at churches, conferences, and seminars. Although Dr. Brandt encouraged me to use this method, he warned me that I would help fewer people through this method than through the first three. He agreed, however, that there is tremendous power and effectiveness in preaching.

5. Counsel on a personal basis. This method, although highly effective, helps the least number of people. Dr. Brandt advised me to set up regular counseling sessions, however, because without contact with real people and real problems I'd soon have nothing to say through the other four methods.

In ways beyond my ability to imagine, God eventually opened all five of these doors for me. Within six years from the time I first began "standing in God's line," God began to supernaturally affirm all five. At first I eliminated the thought of writing a book or making a video. Considering my literary abilities and my financial resources, I felt these were out of the question. But the more I thought about how all things are possible through Christ who gives us strength (see Philippians 4:13) and that it was God who wanted me to serve people, I concluded that my attitude limited God. The more I prayed about and studied the five methods Dr. Brandt suggested—books, audio-tapes, videos, speaking, and counseling—the more I sensed a peace about using all five methods myself.

Norma was as excited about the five methods as I was, so together with our children and a few friends we began to pray that before I turned sixty God would allow me to write a book about helping couples stay in harmony. Like the persistent widow in Luke 18, I started every morning in God's line, praying and hoping for the day I would see a book in print. Sometimes I walked into bookstores and imagined my book on the shelf, even though I knew my skills were still inadequate. I didn't expect God to answer my prayer for a number of years, but that didn't diminish my enthusiasm.

While I was standing in God's line many people tried to discourage me by reminding me of how many books have already been written about marriage and of how difficult it is to get a book published. Then they would say, "And almost none of them become best-sellers." They were right; the odds are slim that any one book will sell more than 5,000 to 7,000 copies. They also tried to discourage me from doing a film series because of the popularity of the James Dobson films.

I countered their pessimism and my doubts with the assurance that God was leading me into this. Because God had a unique message to give me, it didn't matter how many books and films were already available. Besides, millions of people needed to be reached, so God could use as many people as he wanted to in order to help people.

I knew I needed a lot of preparation. Whatever your mission and whatever methods you choose to accomplish it, you must learn the necessary skills, even though it may take years. Don't limit yourself and God by dwelling on what you *already* know and can do. We learn best by doing—over and over and over—and if we are faithful in preparing, we will be ready when the opportunity comes. I wanted to be ready when the opportunity came. In other words, as a good friend of mine says, "If God promises you a horse, you'd better start learning to ride!"

Only six months after I started praying, God nearly knocked me off my feet with his first answer. My friend Steve Scott called from Philadelphia and asked if I would let his company finance *two* books by me (one for husbands, the other for wives). He would help me write them, and Pat Boone would endorse them in an advertisement on national television.

The words of Ephesians 3:20 flashed through my mind: "Now to him who is able to do immeasurably more than all we ask or imagine ..." I had prayed for one book, but God gave me an opportunity to write two. I had dreamed of getting one title into bookstores, but God wanted to market my books to a much larger audience through television.

I accepted the opportunity enthusiastically, even though I still considered myself the least likely candidate to write a book. But God is not limited by our inabilities. He does his best work with people who are willing and available to carry out his will of loving others. Willingness is the key; knowledge and skills can be learned.

Although I was a willing student, I had no idea of the amount of time and effort this learning would require. That was especially true of my first two books. Each day I felt as if I were being whipped with a belt. Many times I wondered why I had allowed myself to get into such a pressurized situation—having to produce two books in only a short time. There was a team helping me—at various points seven typists and four ghost-writers were working on the project. Many days I simply concluded, "God, since you opened this door, and because I know you're faithful to your children, I believe you'll enable me to finish what you've started. But I want you to know this is a miserable and painful experience."

While working on the two books, I continued to pray about the other four methods. Before I had finished writing, a producer from Hollywood, California, called to ask if he could send a film crew to Texas to include me in a movie they were producing on strengthening families. In my busyness, I turned down the opportunity without really praying about it. Besides, I'd never heard of the featured pastor in the film, a man by the name of Charles Swindoll. The film, *Strike the Original Match*, became an award winner that still ministers to thousands around the world. God had opened the door I was pounding on, and I had slammed it in his face.

That experience taught me an important lesson. From then on when I knocked, I kept my eyes on the door, expecting it to open at any moment. I felt like the Christians in the book of Acts must have felt when they failed to recognize answered prayer. They were so preoccupied with praying for Peter's release from prison that they didn't believe the servant who told them Peter was knocking on their door (see Acts 12:12–17).

I'm still learning how to recognize God's answers to prayer. For some time I'd prayed about being on *Oprah*. I'd had two small appearances, but then the producer called and asked me to do an entire hour with Oprah about my marriage video. Believe it or not, I asked her if we could do it later? Well, later has never come—yet. But I'm back in line!

Maintenance—Are My Methods Still Effective?

Once we have recognized our mission and are actively pursuing several methods, we'll begin to see which methods are most effective and concentrate on those. In addition, we need to continually ask God to reveal any other methods he wants us to use to accomplish his mission through us.

The first time I heard James Dobson's radio program "Focus on the Family," I realized it would be an effective vehicle to communicate the message God had given me. When I heard reports about the size of Dr. Dobson's audience throughout the world, I got in line before the Lord and asked him for a chance to be a guest so I could share some of the principles of marriage I'd written about in my two books.

The opportunity finally came through a *parenting* book I'd written—*not* the marriage books—but by this time God's unexpected tactics didn't surprise me as much as they had at first. Shortly afterward, John Nieder, the host for a program with Dr. Howard Hendricks of the Center for Christian Leadership at Dallas Theological Seminary, flew to Phoenix to tape some shows with me. John had heard my interview with Dr. Dobson, and he lovingly and sensitively instructed me on how to correct my problem of interrupting the interviewer. I made a sign and placed it on my desk during our interview: DON'T TALK OR MAKE ANY NOISE WHILE JOHN IS SPEAKING. Keeping quiet was difficult, but the memory of my previous humiliation silenced me. I thanked God for loving me enough to give me another opportunity to learn the skills I needed in order to communicate his message more effectively.

Soon after being on Howard Hendricks' program I received the following letter:

I'm writing to you to explain my changing feelings about you over the last several weeks. After I heard you on Dr. Dobson's program, I purposed that I would never listen to you again on radio because you interrupted Dr. Dobson so many times. A friend of mine called me the other day and said you were on Dr. Hendricks' program and it was helping her and I ought to tune in. I told her I could not listen to Mr. Smalley anymore but if she wanted to, that was fine.

But my curiosity got the better of me and I finally turned on the radio. To my amazement, you did not interrupt Mr. Nieder one time. I decided that you must have learned your lesson, and I'm looking forward to hearing you again.

Any relationship, vocation, or ministry, if it is to remain fresh and effective, needs continual evaluation. Do you know why most churches meet at 11:00 A.M. on Sunday mornings? Because a hundred years ago, most church members were farmers and needed time to milk the cows and do their chores before coming to church. Churches that continually reevaluate the times they meet on Sunday (or on other days of the week), the programs they provide for people, and even the method of sermon delivery—all with the idea of better fulfilling their mission—usually have the most exciting and effective ministries. Unfortunately, many get locked into a method and stay with it long after it has served its usefulness, which may indicate they have either forgotten their mission or never knew it.

Mate—Do We Agree About Our Mission?

The last *M* depends on whether we're single or married. For singles, this fits nicely as the final piece in God's plan for life. Once we know our master, mission, and methods, we are much better prepared to decide what type of person we should spend the rest of our lives with. (Or perhaps we may be better prepared to understand why God is calling us to remain single.)

Ideally, discussions about mission and methods should occur before marriage. But often this doesn't happen, and not having done so can produce tension as husband and wife strive to fulfill their own individual missions. I'm not suggesting that marriage partners must have exactly the same mission and methods, but Scripture convinces me that God wants us as equally yoked as possible. I am grateful for a pastor who encouraged me to look for a wife who was going the same direction I was. During our marriage, Norma and I have remained enthusiastic team-mates in our efforts to follow the will of God.

This conclusion may seem obvious, but many people believe they can marry simply on the basis of being "in love" with each other. Later they may discover that their mate has a mission and several methods that are counterproductive to their own mission and methods.

For those who are married the last *M* concerns entering into *oneness* with our mate. Part of becoming one in marriage is learning to be of one mind. Unfortunately, many Christians determine their mission as if they were still single, never pausing to consider the effect their mission will have on their mate and children. Choosing a mission or a method without consulting family members can weaken a family. I've met writers who feel compelled to write regardless of the resistance they feel from their spouse or children. Mission and methods must be determined *with* our spouse if we're married. The oneness we gain is a tremendous asset in helping us fulfill God's will.

Because Norma and my children were part of the praying and planning process, they supported my work when I had to be away from home or when I was working under tight deadlines. And they had the freedom to tell me when I needed to get away from my work in order to spend more time with them.

That wasn't always the case early in our marriage, because I had locked Norma out of my work, especially when I was working with Bill Gothard. But when my fledgling ministry to couples started to expand right about the time our children were getting older, Norma saw an opportunity to join in partnership with me. She started working in the office, even though she didn't really need to work for financial reasons. She wanted to work because she wanted to serve employees and volunteers who help in our seminars, and because she had the detailed administrative skills for this type of work—skills that I lacked. What a gift it has been to work together in this way!

The importance of oneness in marriage was demonstrated recently when I wanted to hire additional staff members for our organization. Norma was hesitant about hiring any new staff; she wanted to continue as a mom-and-pop operation. She was afraid that hiring more people would take more of my time away from home. This disagreement forced us to reexamine our ministry and our time together as a family. After considering the family's needs first and together planning how to keep our family life healthy should we decide to bring on more staff, we were able to go ahead and hire additional employees. But we agreed to certain guidelines so that each of Norma's concerns about our relationship and our family would be honored. As she saw my commitment to oneness with her, she remained as committed as I was to our mission and methods.

The five *M*s have proved to be the final ingredients in my search for the fulfilling life. For many years, I sought fulfillment not only from people and things but from doing good spiritual activities. Though my work helped people, my motivation was wrong: I was expecting worthwhile activities to fill my life. When I recognized that activities, no matter how noble, could *never* permanently satisfy me, I began to allow God to fill me with his joy and love. That's when my needs were truly met. Free to serve others in love, I began to experience overflow, and with few exceptions, my joy has spilled over ever since.

CHAPTER TWELVE

Uncovering Five Secrets of Answered Prayer

WHEN I FIRST THOUGHT about writing this book, I intended it to help people learn to deal with trials and to see how Jesus Christ energizes our life. Now I realize I've actually written a book about building a relationship with God through prayer. The context we're looking at is marriage, but these truths will aid anyone in their relationship with God, regardless of whether they are married and regardless of whether their spouse chooses to look to God for life or not.

When I began my search for the source of life, I expressed my desire in a prayer: "God, teach me what I am missing." When I took my personal retreat, all the lessons I learned through Scripture related to prayer. I realized that *persistence*—getting in God's line every day—was the secret to experiencing the fulfilling life God promised. Next I recognized that my negative emotions were warning lights that showed me I was expecting to find life's meaning in God's creation rather than in the Creator. Prayer corrected each of those emotions. Trials motivated me to treasure hunt—through prayer. And my search to find and implement God's mission and methods for my life has led me even deeper in prayer.

Perhaps some of us think of prayer only as words of thanks we mutter before eating, as a ritual performed during a Sunday morning worship service, as clichés spoken during family devotions, or as cries for help in the face of a major crisis. These are valid occasions for prayer, to be sure, but there is so much more. Prayer is what connects us to the source of life that charges our batteries and makes life worth living. When both husband and wife have this kind of life, the result is *joy,* as God intended it in marriage.

Is it really that simple? Is prayer all we need to have a fulfilling life? In some ways, a prayer life is like a puzzle made for preschoolers: It contains only a few pieces. Some people, however, delight in cutting each piece into smaller pieces so that it takes years of education and experience to assemble the puzzle. Although understanding increases as we mature, newborn believers can experience through prayer the joy of a fully energized, overflowing life just as those who have known God for many years.

Although we could never explore every aspect of prayer in one chapter, or even in an entire book, the following thoughts explain what I believe it means to *pray effectively.*

Prayer—Rehearsing God's Will

As the Israelites prepared to enter the Promised Land, Moses warned them not to forget all that God had commanded. Since Canaan had no thriving religious book publishing industry to preserve the law in writing, the Israelites taught God's commands to their children from morning until night—as they sat in their homes, as they walked to and from work, as they went to sleep, and as they rose in the morning (see Deuteronomy 6:1–9). Every day they reviewed and reminded each other of God's laws.

Like the Israelites who rehearsed God's law, I believe an important aspect of prayer is *rehearsing God's will*. Regularly reminding ourselves of God's will keeps us pointed toward God's goal and helps us learn what it means to value him and others. It makes us ask questions like, "Whom am I going to love today?" "Whom will I encourage?" "Have I offended anyone from whom I need to ask forgiveness?" It points out my selfishness and reveals my need to continually turn away from my selfish ways and show compassion to those around me, particularly my spouse, by becoming a channel of God's love.

Rehearsing God's will also requires that I keep my mission in front of me. All successful corporations set clearly defined objectives that determine their day-to-day business strategies. Jesus taught this principle in the Sermon on the Mount: "But seek first his kingdom and his righteousness, and all these things will be given to you as well" (Matthew 6:33). Norma and I allow God to set the goals that will further his kingdom, then we go to him daily, praying for the opportunities and necessary resources to reach those objectives.

The most important aspect of rehearsing God's will is making sure we pray only for things that are consistent with 1 Timothy 6:3–4: "If anyone teaches false doctrines and does not agree to the sound instruction of our Lord Jesus Christ and to godly teaching, he is conceited and understands nothing." These verses apply to false teachers, but I use them to double-check my prayer life. Is my prayer consistent with what Jesus taught? Will what I am praying for lead to godliness?

But successful prayer requires more than knowing God's will. It also requires *faith*, and I have found that my faith works best when I mentally picture what I'm praying for.

Prayer—Picturing God's Desires

In an earlier chapter I cited two contrasting examples of faith: the Roman soldier who exhibited *great* faith, and the disciples crossing the Sea of Galilee who exhibited *little* faith (see Matthew 8:5–13, 23–27). When the storm raged around the disciples, they were afraid of losing their lives, even though Jesus had told them they were going to the other side of the lake (see Matthew 8:18). The waves crashing over their boat washed away their vision of a safe arrival on the opposite shore. Great faith is knowing, even in the midst of a storm, that we will reach the destination God has given us. Great faith has confidence that it's only a matter of time—a few days, a few years—until we reach God's goals.

Having great faith is impossible without a picture of God's goals in our minds. We need to *see* how we should act with Jesus Christ in our life. All of us who know God personally should obey his commands to love him, value ourselves, and be concerned for the welfare of others. God wants our lives to display the fruit of the Spirit (Galatians 5:22–23). How will we act when we are loving, joyful, peaceful, patient, kind, good, faithful, gentle, and self-controlled?

We each need to talk with our spouse about people we know who exhibit the fruit of the Spirit. We should be able to point to someone and say, "That person has life. That's what I want to be like." Although we must not place our expectations for a fulfilling life in humans, we need examples of men and women totally dedicated to God. The director of a powerful Christian ministry in Europe sets a living example for me of how God can shine through us. He exudes life. His facial expressions, warm friendly greetings, and, most of all, his contagious enthusiasm all convey his total love for Jesus. He helps me *see* what Romans 8:29 means when it says that God's desire is for me to become like God's Son, Jesus Christ.

Al and Jo like to look for couples in their church who model a godly marriage. When the Janssens were young parents living in Salem, Oregon, they became friends with Herb and Esther. Herb was a retired veterinarian, and Esther had spent the majority of her married life raising five children. Now that their children were grown, this couple was sold out to ministry—together. Esther taught an adult Sunday School class with Al; Herb served as a deacon.

But their ministry was so much more. Esther enjoyed spending time with newly married women. She spent a full day with Jo in the kitchen teaching her how to can fruit. Herb and Esther constantly opened their home—for dinner, for Bible studies, or for longer stretches to care for people who needed a safe place for a few days or weeks.

The Janssens no longer live in Salem, but they often talk about this couple who modeled how to minister together. They also fondly recall an elderly couple who lived a couple of blocks from them. They were in their late eighties, had been married for sixty-five years, and had never spent a night apart from each other. He was a retired pastor, and this couple spent two hours every morning praying for people in the church. Al and Jo like to say, "We want to be like these two couples when we're 'retired.'"

Another helpful tool is to picture specific commands of Scripture being fulfilled in our lives. Just as we would use a movie camera to record an event so we could watch it as often as we wanted to, our mental cameras can "record" an event we can play back daily to help us understand how God may answer a prayer. For instance, using God's command to "encourage the fainthearted" (1 Thessalonians 5:14, NASB), I picture a scene in much the same way a movie camera would. I may see myself sitting in the living room with a husband and wife who are headed for divorce. They are "fainthearted" and want me to help. I imagine interacting with them, counseling them, and then seeing them emerge from our meeting with renewed hope. If the disciples had done this in Matthew 8, Jesus would have commended them for their great faith. Because they had not "filmed" their arrival on the other shore, they were not able to weather the storm.

God realizes that we need mental pictures in order to grasp his will. When God promised to make Abraham a great nation, he helped Abraham *see* the promise by showing him the stars of heaven. "So shall your offspring be," God promised him (Genesis 15:5). Abraham believed God in spite of one major problem: Abraham had no children. How could he have children as numerous as the stars if his wife couldn't become pregnant? Abraham's "storm" lasted for many years. When the fulfillment of that promise was delayed, Sarah tried to help God by having Abraham father a son by her servant Hagar, which proved to be a major disaster. We should beware of running ahead of God's plan and trying to "help" him with our ideas of how to achieve the goal.

God, in his faithfulness, finally gave Abraham and Sarah a son when Sarah was ninety years old. But then, inexplicably, God told Abraham to sacrifice his only child. Abraham knew, however, what God had promised so he believed that even if he had to kill his son, God could raise him up again. Abraham trusted God because he had pictured the fulfillment of all God had promised him.

This principle of prayer is so powerful that we must be careful how we use it. We might find ourselves receiving something we never really wanted. A classic illustration is the story of the Israelites who cried out for meat in the desert after God led them out of Egypt (see Numbers 11:4). I can almost hear them chanting, "We want meat! We want meat! We want meat!" It was not God's will for them to have meat; God had already provided manna. But in their stubborn persistence, visualizing the meat they'd had in Egypt, they were relentless. So God gave them meat (see Numbers 11:18), but with it sent "leanness into their soul" (Psalm 106:15, KJV), or "a wasting disease" (Psalm 106:15, NIV). Some translations say they gagged on the meat and vomited all over the desert.

A common "meat-in-the-desert" mental picture is *lust*. When our minds are filled with lustful visions and we imagine the pleasure of lying down with a person other than our spouse, we should be quick to remind ourselves and the Lord that we do *not* want this fulfilled. Certainly there is pleasure in sin, but only for a short time. Most of us do not realize the devastating effects of extramarital sexual relationships. I once heard a pastor pray candidly, "Please, Lord, I never want this vision fulfilled. I do not want to trade the joy of a fulfilling life for the pain of sexual diseases, a calloused soul, a devastated wife, a ruined ministry, loss of self-control, and all the other consequences I don't even know right now. The price is too high."

To protect my prayers I refer again to Psalm 37:4: "Delight yourself in the LORD and he will give you the desires of your heart." God is number one in my life; God is also number one in Norma's life. No person or thing is of more value to either of us than knowing God. Consequently, the most important activity in our lives is spending time with him. As each of us get to know God better, we have found that he, through his Spirit in us, gives each of us specific desires for expressing love to others. There are no limits to what God can do through those who are dedicated to him.

God could have developed in me a desire to serve at a mission outpost in Alaska or in an inner-city ministry. He could have called me to continue pastoring or to be a businessman who could support other ministries. The needs around the world are limitless, and God leads his children to love others through an incredible variety of helping ministries. Some serve through a full-time vocation, others through volunteer efforts, and still others give financial and prayer support. Through prayer, we commit to God the specific desires he gives us. Once I'm convinced God is leading me toward a specific ministry, I begin to pray and picture how he might fulfill the desires he has given me.

Though we're eager to see our desires fulfilled, sometimes we, like Abraham, have to wait to see the results of our faith. In the early 1980s, I had a tremendous desire to film my marriage seminar and make it available to couples all over the world. I didn't read in Scripture, "Gary Smalley, thou shalt produce a film series." Over a period of several months, however, I asked God about this area and carefully considered if a film would put too much strain on my family or violate any section of Scripture. I also sought the counsel of several Christian leaders. When I finally felt a peaceful confidence that this project would honor God and help his children, I began standing in God's prayer line each day.

That's when I started using my imagination, following the direction of Hebrews 11:1 "Now faith is being sure of what we hope for"—I hoped to see this film series helping families— "and certain of what we do not see"—I could not hold the film in my hand, but I could see the evidence in my mind. Hundreds of times, while I jogged early in the morning, I saw myself standing under the hot lights as a camera crew filmed my marriage seminar. As I mentally lived those film sessions, I also prayed, "Lord, remove the peace if this isn't your will. I only want to see this happen because I believe it will help your people. But if it isn't your will, I'll be glad to step out of line and take my request with me."

Though I never had to step out of line, there were at least two false alarms. One film company wanted me and my board of directors to invest a large sum of money before they filmed. None of us had peace about that. On another occasion, a video company actually filmed my seminar. Apparently they either didn't like it or they ran into some technical difficulties, because they never used it. When these opportunities did not materialize, I got right back into God's line. "Lord," I'd pray, "I really thought this was the answer to my prayer. But apparently it was a false alarm." Then I rethreaded the film in my mind and started running it again day after day, confident that we were going to reach "the other side of the lake." I always believed that before I turned sixty my seminar would be on film. But I always remembered, "Lord, I don't need this film to have fullness in you."

What a joy it was when God began to open this door to videotape my seminar sessions. Then my friend Steve Scott with American Telecast hired Dick Clark to promote the series in an infomercial. Now my prayers had never included Dick Clark, or any other celebrity. But I did pray that thousands of couples would be helped by the series, and having a well-known entertainer involved was a tremendous way to get people exposed to this message.

Those days were exciting, but they also required a great deal of work. We spent twelve hours filming the infomercial. I was battling the flu, and I had taken some antihistamine for the sessions, which made my mouth feel like cotton. I remember sitting on the set between takes, thinking about how Scott was risking $150,000 on this project, and feeling very anxious. So I prayed, "Lord, you brought this about, and now I've got the flu. Somehow you have to make this happen, because I can't do it." Though I knew we'd make it to the other side, there were times when I got so seasick from being tossed around that I could hardly wait for the storm to end.

Let me say that just because I see how God may answer a prayer doesn't mean God is obligated to do it my way. My mental images are only *handles* to help me grasp God's promises and his will. The actual fulfillment is God's responsibility, and he often does it differently—and so much better—than I imagined. As I seek him daily, however, making sure I have his desires and believe him for those desires, I can be assured of one thing: God answers the persistent prayers of his children (see Luke 11:1–13).

Before we leave this section, let me suggest a few cautions. There is a form of mental picturing—some call it "visualization"—that could become an attempt to control our own lives *independently* from what God would want. As I have mentioned before, *God's Word* is what guides us at all times. My mental pictures in no way supersede Scripture. They simply do for me what Jesus' parables did for the disciples. They make God's promises as vivid and real as possible.

Today there is a need to biblically balance our understanding of what it means to "picture" something in prayer. On the one hand, some leaders encourage us to picture ourselves as fabulously wealthy, promising that if we *see* ourselves that way, we will be. Although the picture may come easily to mind, with all the biblical injunctions against storing up treasures on earth it is difficult to believe that such a goal could be from God.

On the other hand, some condemn as "psychologically based" and ultimately "satanic in origin" any form of picturing things in our minds. If this judgment is taken too seriously it could frighten us away from using word pictures to strengthen our faith, a method that has encouraged believers, such as King David, throughout history.

When David sought to capture God's presence during times of deepest trial, the Holy Spirit inspired him to use emotional word pictures. For thousands of years Christians have found comfort in picturing the truths of Psalm 23: "The LORD is my shepherd, I shall not be in want. He makes me lie down in green pastures, he leads me beside quiet waters" (Psalm 23:1–2). Is it wrong to "envision" God as our shepherd? How can a person read these verses and not do exactly that?

A picture paints a thousand words, we often say, and we have many pictures in Scripture to turn to. The Lord is pictured as our rock, our shield, our fortress, our counselor, our rear guard, our gate, and our shepherd, to name only a few. In Revelation 5, Christ himself is pictured as both a lion and a lamb.

Sometimes I make up my own word pictures: God is my lawyer who defends me against unjust accusations. He is my architect who designs a shelter that meets my needs. He is my best friend to whom I can tell anything without fear of rejection. He is my gardener who provides all the nutrients I need. He is my life preserver who keeps me afloat during life's storms. He is my shelter who protects me when battles rage. He is my bodyguard who shields me from attacks.

People can abuse mental pictures by either attributing too much power and significance to them or by denying their usefulness altogether. To forbid believers to picture the Lord as their shepherd is a tragic error. We don't ever want to go beyond what God wills or expresses in his Word, but neither do we want to abandon a method of encouragement God has graciously provided.

Using word pictures or any other "magic formula" will not catapult us to instant spirituality. There is no substitute for a day-by-day, personal walk with Jesus Christ. Methods can be practical handles, but they can never solve all our problems. Only through persistent prayer and by spending time in God's Word day by day, year by year, can we grow and develop in our love and understanding of God.

Prayer—Anticipating Answers

Imagine a seven-year-old boy early on a Christmas morning. His parents sneak into his room and gently shake him awake so he can join the family in their Christmas celebration. His eyes open, but with a big yawn, he says, "Mom, since I was up so late last night can I sleep for another hour or two? You can open your gifts without me; I'll join you later."

Is this what happens? Of course not. The child has anticipated this moment for weeks. He's probably pulling his parents out of bed, impatient to find out what's in the packages under the tree. He has shaken them and examined their shapes, trying to guess what they might contain. He can hardly wait to rip off the ribbons and tear through the wrapping paper.

For me, every day is a little like Christmas. I try to approach God in prayer like a seven-year-old on Christmas morning. I've prayed some of my prayers for years, yet each day I "get in line" with enthusiastic anticipation, asking, "Is today the day, Lord?" All day I wait to see if one or more prayers might be answered. And when they are, I often receive two packages when I only asked for one. But that only doubles the overflow, for my battery is being charged by God every day, no matter how many packages I receive—one, two, or none.

Sometimes when I'm reviewing a "Scripture verse film" in my mind, the lightbulb burns out or the projector malfunctions. Almost immediately a new film comes into focus declaring that God will not be faithful to hear me again. This "doubting film" is so convincing that if I view it for long, I lose hope—like when I think, "There's no way God can bring joy this time." I try to shut off the "doubting film" as soon as I recognize it, but sometimes it runs for several minutes no matter what I do.

Sometimes the on/off switch fails to work at all. When this happens the only solution is to get up and walk out of the theater. Then later I reenter the theater of faith and restart the Scripture verse film. In this case, I'm big on reruns.

What is doubt? Put simply, it is *negative faith*. Doubt is allowing a film to run through our minds that says, "This will never happen to me" or "God can't do this in my life" or "I don't deserve this." Doubt is stepping out of God's line. Doubt is Jesus' disciples saying, "We'll never make it to the other side." Doubt is the widow giving up and declaring she will never receive justice. Imagine if she had gone before the judge for one hundred straight days and then given up hope. She would never have known that had she gone one more day the judge would have granted her request—just to get her out of his hair!

Faith, on the other hand, is the "being sure of what we hope for and certain of what we do not see" (Hebrews 11:1). In other words, it is believing that my film imagining the future God desires will eventually become reality. Scripture provides numerous examples. We've already seen how Abraham believed

God's promise. Abel, Enoch, and Noah are three more in a long list. Their faith held firm even though God's promises were not fulfilled during their lifetimes. "All these people were still living by faith when they died. They did not receive the things promised; they only saw them [in their minds] and welcomed them from a distance" (Hebrews 11:13).

One thing about infomercials is that individually they do run their course and something else invariably becomes "hot." After my successful infomercial with Dick Clark, American Telecast hit the jackpot with superstar singer and actress Cher, who was marketing hair care and facial cream. As I watched sales soar for these products, I can honestly say I wasn't jealous or envious. But I did get in line and pray: "God, how come these products are so successful and mine isn't anymore? I have information that could help save marriages and prevent children from suffering the pain of divorce. You've done this before, but there are still so many couples who need help. God, can we find a new celebrity so we could do the infomercial again with my new material on marriage? And could you make it twice as successful as Cher's beauty products?"

Now I was embarrassed to tell anyone about this prayer, especially after the failure of the parenting infomercial. But I prayed this prayer every day, several times a day, and wondered when God would answer.

For months I prayed about the new infomercial. Then one day, Steve Scott called me and couldn't wait to tell me the news: "Gary, I just talked to Connie Selecca and John Tesh, and they're interested in representing you and your new marriage material. They've been watching your videos and it's helped their own relationship. Are you open to that?" Steve didn't know about my prayers. Trying to be calm, but probably acting more like the kid on Christmas morning, I shouted out, "I'd love it!"

It's a good thing I didn't know that only one infomercial in two hundred makes money—although I'm not sure it would have changed my prayer at all, because my faith was in God and in seeing him use me to help marriages. And if God chose to do it, there were no odds against him. The way this goes is after the infomercial is recorded, it's tested in a couple of markets to see how it will work. Steve had no idea how I'd been praying when he called to tell me the test was a fantastic success. "Gary, it's pulling twice as many responses as Cher's infomercial!" Inside, I released an explosion of thanks to the Lord. That was exactly what I'd prayed for!

Of course, in time the Connie Selecca and John Tesh infomercial ran its course. Now I'm in line again for another celebrity couple. I can hardly wait to meet them.

Prayer—Listening to God

Prayer is two-way communication. Just as true friendship requires equal participation from each member, so it is in our relationship with God. We cannot experience the fullness of Jesus Christ if *we* do all the talking. We must also allow God to express his love, will, and truth to us. We can listen to him in many ways, but the three I use most often are reading the Word, picturing it, and waiting for God's peace.

God's Word grabbed my attention one morning as I read verse 1 of James 3. It warned that God will judge teachers more strictly than others. God immediately had my attention. "We all stumble in many ways," the Bible said (James 3:2), but those who are able to control what they say are perfect, able to control their whole bodies. James used three word pictures to explain. First, the small bit put into a horse's mouth determines the direction the two-thousand-pound animal will go. Second, a small rudder determines the course of a large ship. And third, a small spark can ignite a fire that consumes a whole forest. Our tongues are like the bit, the rudder, and the spark.

James 3:8 confused me, however. No one can tame the tongue, it said. I wondered why God would say that those who control their tongues are mature and then say that no one can tame the tongue. I continued reading into chapter 4. In verses 6–10, God revealed the secret of tongue control. James writes that God gives his grace only to the humble—those who recognize their dependence on God and allow his power to control them—and that he opposes the proud. God's grace is power in us to control our tongue, but he only gives grace to the humble.

Now that was only part of the equation. James continued by saying that if we humble ourselves in God's presence, recognizing our complete dependence on him, God will exalt us. In other words, he will lift us to maturity, which will be reflected in a controlled tongue.

Picturing God's Word in our minds, the second aspect of listening to God, helps us become familiar with a verse, a passage, a chapter, even an entire book in the Bible. It is especially helpful when we don't have access to a Bible.

I try to picture God's Word when I'm out running or have some idle time. One morning I read the story of how Jesus healed the woman who touched the hem of his garment (see Luke 8:43–48). Later that day I imagined being at the scene, bringing it to life on my mental screen. I felt and smelled the people pressing around us. I heard the beggars shouting. I saw the lame pushing and shoving, trying to get through the crowd to see Jesus. I heard Jesus ask who touched him, and I watched the woman tremble as she came forward. I heard Jesus speak to her: "Daughter, your faith has healed you. Go in peace." Like the disciples, I wondered how Jesus could have felt one woman's touch among such a crowd. I glimpsed Jesus' sensitivity—he cared for someone I and the others had ignored. I saw faith and love firsthand.

Picturing God's Word also helps us *apply* Scripture. Recently Norma and I have tried to listen to God regarding the painful swelling she has experienced in her knees. Doctors cannot explain the problem. Many Christians have prayed for her, yet she continues to suffer. We can relate to Paul, who three times asked God to relieve him of what many believe was a physical problem (see 2 Corinthians 12:7–10). His problem made him weak, and Norma feels a similar weakness. But Paul also listened to God. In verse 9 the Lord said, "My grace is sufficient for you, for my power is made perfect in weakness." Paul responded, "Therefore I will boast all the more gladly about my weaknesses [rather than boast about himself], so that Christ's power may rest on me. That is why, for Christ's sake, I delight in weaknesses, in insults, in hardships, in persecutions, in difficulties. For when I am weak, then I am strong" (2 Corinthians 12:9–10). Weakness humbles us—and God's grace strengthens the humble.

In his weakness, Paul obtained God's strength—not just for his physical problem, but in numerous circumstances—which sounds like treasure to me! Because of that truth, Norma and I pray something like this: "Lord, we've asked you many times to heal Norma's knees. You've neither healed them nor given us direction as to how to continue praying. So we'll keep asking for direction. Like Paul we agree that your grace is sufficient, for power is being perfected within Norma because of her weakness. We are, therefore, grateful for the weakness, knowing that the power of Christ is dwelling in us."

Another way to listen to God is to wait for his peace. A few years ago, while out jogging, I passed by a new development where each lot has a beautiful, panoramic view of Phoenix. One lot in particular caught my attention. It was expensive, but I figured I could save up for it.

Norma and I got in line, praying that God would allow us to purchase the lot so we could build our dream home. Although we never had complete peace about it, I continued to pray. Finally, when we had saved enough money, I checked with the owner and learned that the lot had tripled in price. Finding this out forced us to reevaluate God's will in our lives. Norma and I determined that God's will for us at that time was to use our income for ministry purposes, not to pursue a new home. With that settled, we were free and at peace to stay where we were.

The peace of Christ should "rule in [our] hearts" (Colossians 3:15). The meaning of the Greek word translated *rule* is "to function like an umpire." Peace, or lack of it, is one way God has of telling us whether we are *out* or *safe,* and whether a situation is *fair* or *foul.* This does not mean we can never make a decision until we feel some kind of mystical peace. Some people, by their very nature, would never make any decision if they had to wait until they felt peace about it. It means instead that we can be at peace about doing the things God's Word specifically says we should do. For instance, God says we should go to a brother or sister we've offended and ask for forgiveness. Therefore we can have peace about doing that even though we may feel anything but peaceful on the way over to do it.

As we experience God's peace, as we hear him speak to us through Scripture, and as we see his answers to prayer, we will be motivated to worship and praise him even more.

Prayer—Praise and Worship

In the chapters on treasure hunting we discussed one aspect of praise—being *grateful* for trials—but praise and worship involve many other areas, such as singing praise songs, expressing gratitude for God's love and generous gifts, and gathering together with fellow Christians for group expressions of our love for God. Praise and worship recognize the magnitude of God's great worth. Praising God motivates us to express his love to others: "My command is this: Love each other as I have loved you" (John 15:12).

In the twenty-plus years since I've learned to get in line and petition God about the things I know he cares about, I've seen some remarkable answers to prayer. Sometimes the answers just keep coming and coming, far more than I ever hoped for or dreamed of. That was the case with the infomercial I taped with John Tesh and Connie Selecca. We had six videos for those who signed up, and normal response rates predicted that by the sixth month most subscribers would have dropped out. But that wasn't happening. Steve called me to say, "I need you to record seven brand-new sessions. You've got four months to develop and record this material."

Now that may sound like an exciting opportunity, except for this little fact—I'd covered just about all of my material in the first six videos. "God, this is going to take a miracle," I prayed. "Only you can do this." I rested in God as I asked for input from four experts, all friends of mine—Dr. Gary Oliver, Dr. Dan Trathen, Dr. Rod Cooper, and Dr. Ken Canfield. They helped me develop the seven new sessions, which were taped in Denver.

The new videos kept nearly 300,000 subscribers in the club. Many others couldn't wait for a new video each month; they ordered all thirteen at once. I couldn't help but praise God for his goodness. Then Steve called again and said he needed six more sessions because people weren't dropping out. I laughed out loud, sure he was joking this time. He wasn't!

People kept right on ordering. A new infomercial was filmed, and orders kept pouring in. How can I do anything but worship and praise God for the incredible things he has done through me to help marriages around the world? I feel I'm one of the least qualified to teach this material. My speaking skills are certainly very average. The only things I have to offer are my enthusiasm, my vulnerability, and my transparency. And the reason I can be vulnerable and transparent is because *God is my source of life.* So I'm free to admit my failures, and that seems to be what causes people to be attracted to me and my ministry.

When I got in line and asked God to give me opportunity to minister to hurting couples, I couldn't have imagined how God would use these messages. More than six million videos have been distributed around the world. Every ship in the United

States Navy has a set of videos. The Pentagon has bought a set for every Air Force base, as well as for many army bases. Thousands of churches use the videos for premarriage counseling of engaged couples. And this doesn't begin to cover what God has done through the marriage books.

All I can say is that the reason this has happened is because *God* opened the door. God gave the power. God provided the wisdom and insight. God energized my battery and gave me the very life I needed to do this. Therefore, all the success of the videos and books is in his hands. I can never take credit for it. The moment I start thinking it has something to do with me, I notice that the joy leaves. And after knowing this joy, I can't live for very long without it!

Prayer undoubtedly encompasses many other areas, areas I am not confident to discuss today, areas I may not experience until I reach old age. But my desire is for you to experience at least the degree of fullness Norma and I have in Christ, to know at least as much as we know of his love, and to experience at least the level of joy and peace he's given us. That will provide us with plenty of reasons to praise and worship our Creator God.

EPILOGUE

AT ITS CORE, THIS book is about *knowing and loving God—* individually, and as married couples—and *loving people.* In the process of doing that, we experience joy. However, learning to love God and others and experiencing this joy can take a life-time. God has allowed Norma and me to experience some tri-als in recent years that have enabled us to go deeper in our walk with God and in the depth of our love for people.

One of our biggest trials was when our counselors (financial, professional, and staff) all told us we needed to do an audit of the company that had produced the infomercials and videos. Their reasoning made good sense—over the years errors in roy-alties often occur, and my contract allows for such an examina-tion. What I never anticipated was how it would affect our relationship that was built on trust. After a lot of hurt feelings, I decided I had to stop the audit.

About this same time, there was a misunderstanding with a ministry leader. What's more, there was embarrassing publicity about the celebrity couple in one of our infomercials. All of these caused Norma and me to draw closer together. The reality of the message of this book was tested—and again God proved stronger than any problem we faced.

All three of these trials have been resolved, but no doubt there will be others in the future. They do not frighten us, because I believe God will use them for good in our lives. Our problems often produce sadness and grief, but we've discovered that the joy we experience in God and in our relationship transcends any current problems.

At the start of this book, I noted five things I needed. In time, I learned that Norma needed those five things. In fact, every individual and every couple needs these same things.

First, Norma and I needed an energy source to recharge our spiritual and emotional batteries. We found that source in God himself. We have learned that we will gain no lasting energy from people, things, or career. Instead, we have learned to go to Jesus Christ for all of our needs. The couple who discovers this truth is on the road to finding lasting joy.

Second, Norma and I needed someone to whom we could pour out our hearts and to whom we could talk about anything at any time. Again, that person turned out to be God, and we have discovered that this Friend is available to us twenty-four hours a day through prayer. It's interesting, though, that as our prayer life has improved, so has our communication as husband and wife. The intimacy we desired in our marriage has actually occurred—once we stopped expecting it from each other.

Third, Norma and I needed to understand our negative emotions, for they were error messages telling us when we were in trouble. Like any couple, we've had our times of hurt feelings, envy, and anger. For years, our relationship seemed to rise and fall according to our emotions—until we learned that our emotions were our own individual responsibility, not our spouse's. When we began to recognize how our emotions revealed our own selfishness, we were able to use that information to return to God, the source of life, to meet our needs, and those emotions quickly dissipated.

Fourth, Norma and I needed to know there is meaning in the trials we endure. What a joy it has been to learn that trials can produce gold, if we are willing to search for it. Any individual can do this, but when we do it as a couple, there is tremendous benefit to a marriage.

Fifth, Norma and I needed to have a shared mission that was beyond us, one that we could strive for together. As wonderful as my work was with Bill Gothard, it was always my work, not Norma's. Today our ministry is a joint work. I cannot do what I do in public if she doesn't do what she does in the office and at home. Our ministry is a union of our gifts, with a result that many thousands of marriages have been helped. That union of mission and method has produced tremendous joy.

It is my prayer that every one of you would realize that your joy and peace and fulfillment is not dependent on God's creation, but on Jesus Christ himself. As couples, let's look to the Creator, loving him with all our heart, soul, mind, and strength. As he meets our needs, let's look for ways to fulfill his command to love others.

For those who feel cheated by life or disillusioned in this relationship with God, I trust this book will be a freshly paved path leading you to a full and lasting relationship with the giver of life, our Lord Jesus Christ.

SUGGESTED READING

Carlson, Dwight L. *Overcoming Hurts and Anger.* Eugene, Ore.: Harvest House, 1981.

Crabb, Larry. *Men and Women: Enjoying the Difference.* Grand Rapids: Zondervan, 1993.

Curtis, Brent, and John Eldredge. *The Sacred Romance: Drawing Closer to the Heart of God.* Nashville: Thomas Nelson, 1997.

Lawrence, Brother. *The Practice of the Presence of God: Conversations and Letters of Brother Lawrence.* Boston: Oneworld Publications, 1999.

May, Gerald G. *Addiction and Grace: Love and Spirituality in the Healing of Addictions.* New York: HarperCollins, 1991.

Minirth, Frank, and Paul Meier. *Happiness Is a Choice.* Grand Rapids: Baker, 1994.

Murray, Andrew. *Humility: The Beauty of Holiness.* Fort Washington, Pa.: Christian Literature Crusade, 1997.

Nouwen, Henri. *The Way of the Heart: Desert Spirituality and Contemporary Ministry.* San Francisco: HarperSanFrancisco, 1991.

Peck, M. Scott. *The Road Less Traveled.* New York: Simon and Schuster, 1998.

McVey, Steve. *Grace Walk.* Eugene, Ore.: Harvest House, 1995.

McVey, Steve. *Grace Rules.* Eugene, Ore.: Harvest House, 1998.

Warren, Neil Clark. *Finding Contentment: When Momentary Happiness Just Isn't Enough.* Nashville: Thomas Nelson, 1997.

WOMEN OF FAITH℠

Women of Faith partners with various Christian organizations,
including Zondervan Publishing House, Campus Crusade for
Christ International, CleanWeb, Integrity Music, International
Bible Society, New Life Clinics, New Life Ministries,

Partnerships, Inc., Power and Glory, Remuda Ranch, *Today's
Christian Woman* magazine, and World Vision to
provide spiritual resources for women.

For more information about Women of Faith
or to register for one of our nationwide conferences,
call 1-800-49-FAITH.

www.women-of-faith.com

*For more information about the ministry
of Gary Smalley, contact*

The Smalley Relationship Center
800-848-6329
or
www.garysmalley.com

Bring Home the Joy

Best-Selling Authors Share the Secrets of Adding Enjoyment and Vitality to Your Marriage

Larry Crabb, Dr. Kevin Leman, Les and Leslie Parrott, Gary Smalley, Roger and Becky Tirabassi, and Neil Clark Warren

Bring Home the Joy offers a "best of the best" collection of published writings from some of today's most sought-after relationship specialists. This insightful book will help strengthen and renew marriages at every stage. Whether you and your mate are newlyweds, parents of kids from toddlers to teens, empty nesters, or marriage veterans celebrating a golden anniversary, *Bring Home the Joy* will bring greater strength and intimacy to your relationships—both with each other and with God.

Hardcover 0-310-22786-0
Softcover 0-310-23448-4

How to Become Your Husband's Best Friend

Gary Smalley

This excerpt from the best-seller *For Better or For Best* offers practical advice to help wives gain the kind of relationship with their husbands they would love to have.

Pick up your copy today at your local Christian bookstore!

Mass Market 0-310-44992-8

For Better or For Best

A Valuable Guide to Knowing, Understanding, and Loving Your Husband

Gary Smalley

A how-to-book for women that outlines the steps wives can take to gain better marriages and shows the emotional and motivational differences between men and women.

Softcover 0-310-44871-9
Mass Market 0-310-21467-X

If Only He Knew

A Valuable Guide to Knowing, Understanding, and Loving Your Wife

Gary Smalley

A how-to book for men that clarifies the distinctions between men and women with a view toward building a stronger marital relationship.

Softcover 0-310-44881-6
Mass Market 0-310-21478-5

Hidden Keys to a Loving, Lasting Marriage

(formerly *The Joy of Committed Love*)

Gary Smalley

Best-selling author Gary Smalley shares his principles for strong marriages in this book that combines the practical insights of *If Only He Knew* and *For Better or For Best*.

Pick up your copy today at your local Christian bookstore!

Softcover 0-310-40291-3

We want to hear from you. Please send your comments about this book to us in care of the address below. Thank you.

ZondervanPublishingHouse
Grand Rapids, Michigan 49530
http://www.zondervan.com